LOOK FOR RAINBOWS

For the sad, the lonely, the depressed and the despairing

Gateway Books, Bath

First published in 1987
by GATEWAY BOOKS
The Hollies, Wellow,
Bath, BA2 8QJ

Second Printing 1988

Distributed in the U.S.A. by
SLAWSON COMMUNICATIONS
2719 Sixth Avenue,
San Diego, CA 92103

cover artist: Chrissie Snelling
cover design: Studio B, Bristol

Set in 11/12½ pt. Sabon by
Mathematical Composition Setters Ltd,
of Salisbury
Printed by WBC Print of Bristol,

British Library Cataloguing in Publication Data:
   Gibson, Joan
     Look for rainbows: for the sad,
     the depressed and the despairing.
     1. Depression, Mental
     I. Title
     362.2   RC537

ISBN 0.946551.39.1

LOOK FOR RAINBOWS

Contents

Introduction

There are three great and wonderful qualities bestowed upon every human being at birth, no matter how poor or underprivileged, which, by their very nature, lift man onto a higher plane than any other creature in the animal kingdom. They may lie dormant and unrecognised or, if we will, we may seek to use and develop them. It is only through them that we learn to discover more of the ultimate truth about ourselves, about life, and the source of life which most of us call God. We sometimes speak of these attributes as the three great virtues, faith, hope and love. Faith is the recognition of a living power greater than ourselves to which we belong and must respond as a flower turns towards the sun; hope, the belief that there is purpose in all life, that good will prevail over evil, and that life is a journey which is leading us home; and love, the greatest of all these gifts to mankind, which is the knowledge of God himself within us transforming our lives and enabling us to love in our turn the world and its beauty, our fellow human beings, and God, our creator, from whom we came and to whom we will return.

None of the three can ever be wholly lost or destroyed; they burn like inextinguishable bright sparks deep within us, but it is hope that is all too easily lost sight of when sorrows, cares, fears, doubts and all the other pressures of life crowd in upon us, and we stumble in the darkness, bewildered and afraid, not knowing which way to turn. Yet without hope life has no meaning and we become like mice in a treadmill, working feverishly but accomplishing nothing.

Children never lack hope. We see it shining in their eyes as they joyfully tackle each new experience with confidence and happy expectation. They have learned to trust their parents and know that they are being guided and protected. It is as we grow older, as we find that we must stand on our own feet, bear the responsibilities of life, cope with danger, failure and our own inadequacies, and as we must contend with illness, grief and loss, that sometimes our feet falter and we feel that our burdens are too great to bear.

I was standing in a busy railway station recently watching the crowds pass by. So many faces were strained, fearful, weary and drawn; so many shoulders bowed. It seemed that only the young were carefree. Yet the world is incredibly beautiful and to be alive such a great privilege. We need to rediscover hope, for hope is the most powerful antidote to weariness and despair.

In Ancient Greek mythology all earthly ills and sorrows were first set at large when the nymph Pandora, overcome by curiosity and disobeying the strict instructions of the gods, opened a sealed box which had contained them. But in the same box was imprisoned hope, and hope was able to lessen much of the evil caused by her vindictive companions, so that they were prevented from destroying mankind. The story of Pandora's box is curiously similar to that of Adam and Eve. In both it was disobedience and curiosity which brought evil into the world, and in both humanity was not destroyed utterly, but a door of escape provided. That door was hope.

Life is often considered to resemble a journey and, as we travel, we experience all the vicissitudes to which the wayfarer may be exposed. Hope is surely to be recommended as the best comrade for that journey. Despair is the denial of hope and the false friend to be shunned. Despair will do everything to hamper and delay us; hope gives us courage to go on. When John Bunyan wrote his epic work, *The Pilgrim's Progress*, he described the Slough of Despond in which many travellers perished, and later his pilgrim's most trusted companion was aptly named Hopeful.

So what do we mean by hope? It is no sentimental, saccharine, 'cloud-cuckoo land' mentality which shuts its eyes to wrong-doing and suffering, believing that they will then go away. Hope is a strong, powerful virtue, not a frail etherial spirit. It makes us take positive action rather than weep over our misfortunes. Hope is not blind to the realities of pain and grief, but gives us the courage to accept and endure them. Hope believes that powerful though the forces of evil may be, the forces of good are greater still and will ultimately triumph over them. Hope never falters, never gives up and never fails us. What better friend could we choose to walk with us when we find life's burdens too onerous to bear alone?

> Think not that hope is dead, crushed by your pain,
> As if you grasped a snowflake's fragile form.
> Hope is the star that rides above the storm
> And through its rage clear-shining will remain.
> Those treasured autumn leaves will fall to dust;
> Dreams of the past can only live in sleep
> And happy memory: but can you keep
> Your fettered soul from sorrow by such trust?
> As steady as a lantern's guiding light
> No fickle firefly hope will prove to be.
> Dread not apparent failure; she can see
> Beyond the fearful depth, the awesome height.
> Hope is eternal. Keep her by your side;
> Throughout life's journey trust her as your guide.

In the following chapters I will try to show how hope can still be discovered in however desperate a situation we may find ourselves. It is not easy to believe in hope when we see cause for nothing but despair. It may help us if we think of the farmer ploughing his fields in the depths of a bleak and barren winter, preparing for and believing in the growth of the harvest that is to come. Let us resolve, therefore, to put aside our doubts and fears, to go on with the journey of life, and to plough in hope.

1. I'm so Lonely – No one Ever Speaks to Me

This can be a real cry of despair. To be confined within four walls day after day with nothing to relieve the monotony, where the tick of the clock only emphasises the impossibly slow and weary passage of time, where the postman passes by and friends forget to call and there is just the dull ache of loneliness for company – this is no way for life to be. Yet many endure such an existence. Loneliness is desperately hard to bear. Walking home to a cold and empty house, after passing lighted windows which reveal tantalising glimpses of happy family activities within, only makes the burden greater. If we are in this situation we must seek a way of escape. And ways can be found.

It is hardest, of course, for the deaf, the disabled and the very old. These people need the help of the various associations which have been set up on their behalf; and much is being done to make life easier for those with specific problems. No one should be afraid or too proud to ask for help.

But for all other lonely people the cure lies within ourselves. We have first to ask ourselves the question, 'Do I really want to be involved with others?' If we are strictly honest some of us would have to admit that we should prefer to impose limitations. We are, perhaps, not outgoing by nature, dislike noisy parties, crowded gatherings and social get-togethers, wishing only for the occasional company of those with similar interests to our own. There is nothing wrong with this, providing we realise that to

envy our extrovert neighbours and try to copy their way
of life would be no answer to the problem. On the other
hand, we cannot impose too many conditions if we wish
to make friends, pushing some people away and only being
willing to associate with others on our own terms. Friendship involves giving as well as taking; we must sometimes
be prepared to give in to others' wishes, to visit them
rather than expect them to call on us, and to be willing to
listen to their point of view. We cannot force people to
befriend us, nor should we feel aggrieved if they do not
respond to our advances; friendship must be earned and
shared.

Having, then, decided that we truly wish to alter our
way of thinking and our mode of life in order to escape
from loneliness, we must set aside the feeling of despair
and look hopefully at what may be done. 'To make a
friend you must be one' is wisely said, but how can this be
brought about? There are a number of steps to take, and
we have to begin by changing ourselves and our whole
outlook on life.

We must make friends with ourselves

People tend to accept us at our own valuation. If we feel
we are poor, worthless creatures we can hardly expect
others to see us as desirable companions. In any case, such
an assessment of ourselves is untrue. We are the worst
judges of our own worth. We are as we were created,
unique persons, inheriting some traits of character from
our ancestors, but with our upbringing and environment
also playing an important part. While we can change
ourselves to some extent, which indeed we are now
endeavouring to do, we cannot alter our basic selves, nor
should we wish to. The world would be dull indeed if we
were all carbon copies of the next person, reacting in the
same way to every situation. There is no sense in blaming
ourselves because we are lonely, or feeling that we are un-
worthy of having friends. We all have our good points and
our weaknesses. It is up to us to make the most of our indi-

viduality; to understand ourselves, accept ourselves, and finally to respect and like the person we are. If we must spend long hours in our own company this is surely essential. Therefore, we must aim to be happy and at peace with ourselves before we can reach out to others.

We must learn how to enjoy solitude

While it is certainly desirable to spend some time with our fellows enjoying the stimulation of their company and conversation, it is equally good for us to experience periods of solitude when we can be free to think our own thoughts and give our minds freedom to relax and meditate. Far from being times of loss, these quiet interludes will help us to become less tense and anxious and will give us a fresh outlook on life. We need to escape sometimes from the noise and turmoil of modern life to discover, as Wordsworth put it, 'the bliss of solitude'; to be able to wander without haste or pressure enjoying the beauty of the earth we inhabit. We must not be afraid of our own thoughts. It is very necessary to use our minds and decide for ourselves what opinions and beliefs we hold. This will develop our own personalities so that, when we do hold conversations with others, we will be eager to hear their ideas and will have interesting points of view of our own to put forward.

There is nothing frightening about being alone with our thoughts, but they must be positive and forward looking. It is pointless to dwell in the past, either regretting actions taken or longing to return to happier days. This can only be a futile exercise, for the past cannot be changed. We may learn from it, but not re-live it. In seeking to meditate we should find a suitable place that is both peaceful and quiet. It may be the hushed atmosphere of a church, a comfortable chair by the window or fireside, a corner in a sunny garden, the river bank or the shade of a tree. Here we can relax and allow our thoughts to wander. But to benefit most we need a focus for our contemplation. Many people will take a Bible verse and allow the words to run through their minds, or they will concentrate on a single object; a flower, a butterfly, or a cloud, absorbing its beauty and perfection. Thoughts like these bring hope and happiness into our hearts.

There are advantages in being alone at times. We are free to go at our own pace, indulge our own whims and fancies, enjoy any personal idiosyncrasy without fear of criticism of ridicule. There are many pursuits for which solitude is a great asset. Watching birds, painting, fishing, and photography to name but a few, can be carried out more satisfactorily alone, and much pleasure and satisfaction can be derived from them. It is worth while, whatever our circumstances, to have at least one pastime which does not require the company of our fellows. We need to develop some measure of independence, so that we are able to find pleasure in our own company when others are not available.

Making friends with Nature

We are never truly alone when we are out of doors; we are but a very small part of the life which teems upon the universe, and fascinating things can be discovered if we will take the time to look about us. Town-dwellers are accustomed to stop, look and listen before crossing busy roads. The same practice should be observed when we are in parks or country lanes; yet, so often, sunk into our gloomy and self-obsessed thoughts, we are blind to the beauties which surround us and pass them by heedless and unseeing.

Once, in early spring, I chanced to walk over the Downs near to my home. I was coping at the time with domestic problems and was wrapped in anxious thought, as I reached a narrow path through a beech wood. All at once I became aware of a strange and very pungent odour, almost like onions, and curious to discover what this could be, I stopped to look at the ground at the side of the path which fell away in a steep slope to fields far below. Under the trees a carpet of wild garlic spread its pure, white, delicate flowers, gleaming above a dark background of fallen leaves as if a whole galaxy of stars had been scattered there. And as I wondered at their sheer brilliance, I also marvelled at the shafts of sunlight filtering through the trees in bands of gold, lighting up the wonderful fresh green of opening beech leaves. Peace and calm seemed to enfold me in that quiet wood and it felt as though a great weight had been lifted from my shoulders, just by allowing myself to become at one for a few moments with the beauty that was about me. Yet I could so easily have passed it by unnoticed.

Plants, flowers, shrubs and trees have no emotions as we know them, but they do share with us the gift of life and, to some extent, we are in harmony with them because of that common bond, so loneliness is less acute if we keep ourselves close to other living things. Many find great consolation in their houseplants, even talking to them and stroking them, which may sound ridiculous, but has the effect of making us more aware of them. Trees especially appear to have a comforting and friendly presence. We shelter beneath them from rain or excessive heat, we may even climb into their branches, we admire their blossom, gain sustenance from their fruit, they enhance the beauty of photographs and paintings and enrich us in so many ways. We see how a tree supports much life apart from its own, providing both food and shelter for other plants, insects, animals and birds. It is small wonder that there has been an outcry against the wanton destruction of trees. Many an ancient and well-loved oak or chestnut has been saved from felling by petitions from those who felt fervently that it must be preserved.

Water in ponds, lakes, streams, rivers or the sea, has no life of its own and yet it, too, has comforting qualities when we are lonely and distressed. Perhaps it is the way in which it maintains other life. Indeed, we are told that life first began in the sea, and a single drop of pond water under a microscope will reveal countless living organisms. Moving water has a particular fascination, and I have

always thought that the stony becks of the northern countries, so clear and sparkling as they cascade over rocks and
pebbles, are especially companionable; the murmur of a
stream is a wonderful soporific. This is why it is so much
easier to be able to relax on a beach, where the continuous
lap and sough of the advancing and receding tide provides
a gentle background music, reminding us subconsciously
perhaps of our mother's heart beat as we lay safe and
protected within her womb.

I found these lines written by Ruskin and inscribed on
his memorial stone by the shore of Lake Derwentwater:

> The spirit of God is around you in the air that you
> breathe, His glory in the light that you see and in the
> fruitfulness of the earth and the joy of its creatures.
> He has written for you day by day His revelation, as
> He has granted you day by day your daily bread.

Making friends with animals

For those who for one reason or another must live alone,
a very obvious palliative to loneliness is to own a pet;
whether it is a cat, dog, bird, mouse or goldfish is a matter
of personal preference. They can be perfect companions,
and caring for them can add purpose to our lives and a
much-needed outlet for love and affection. If, however, it
is not practicable to keep a pet, we may still enjoy observ-
ing and being in touch with the many animals and birds
that throng our towns and countryside. Bird watching is a
fascinating and rewarding hobby, with ever more to learn
and discover. It is possible to befriend town birds, particularly in the winter, by putting food and water where we
may conveniently watch them. The R.S.P.B sell many very
pleasing bird feeders which will attract tits and other rarer
species. Wild animals are understandably wary of human
beings, but although they try to conceal their presence they
are not too difficult to observe. I am always delighted to
see rabbits in the fields; though to glimpse a fox, hare or
stoat is a rarer treat.

We sometimes overlook the very small creatures. I once stood at the borders of a wood sheltering from a sudden shower while awaiting the arrival of a bus. I was intrigued by the antics of a family of field mice, which emerged from a tiny hole in the ground close to my foot and played happily with one another for several minutes before realising that I was there. Another day I watched an industrious little shrew hunting a beetle on a grassy bank. The beetle was soon seized and I heard the crunch of teeth as the shrew grasped its scaly back. The beetle, however, eluded death that day, jerking itself free and weaving its way to safety among stones and roots at the bottom of the bank. The shrew, apparently better equipped to smell than to see, was confused and quite lost her prey. These small dramas are occurring all the time, but unless we are observant and receptive to the world of nature around us, we can miss so much.

Making friends with other lonely people

It is only when we have accepted ourselves as we are, have learned how to come to terms with solitude and appreciate the world about us, that we are ready to reach out in friendship to others. But we still cannot expect the world to flock to our door; the first steps must be ours. We may be hesitant to make the initial approach, fearful of rebuff or indifference and so we wonder how to begin. Most people, we will find, already have their own circle of friends. It is not to them that we should turn, but to others who are lonely and longing for friendship like ourselves. It is strange that we so often fail to recognise our fellow loners. Perhaps it is because we are so afraid of being snubbed or ridiculed that we build a wall about ourselves and become almost unapproachable. This can so easily be mistaken for snobbery or pride.

Lonely people can most readily be noticed in crowds or at social gatherings, trying to preserve a nonchalant appearance, but obviously ill at ease. This is when a word from another single person will often break the ice and will be welcomed with gratitude and relief. There are some, of course, who do wish to remain apart, but this will soon become apparent if, after an opening remark, they are unwilling to continue the conversation. People sitting alone on a park bench, standing in a bus queue, or walking the dog will not usually be offended by a pleasant remark about the weather. Indeed, they may well respond with effusion, so revealing their own loneliness.

We need to observe some caution, however, even so. If we are so hungry for companionship that we seek to monopolise the time of a new acquaintance, we may well stifle that potential friendship at birth. We must consider the other person's wishes and be prepared to listen to his troubles as well as unburdening our own, much as we may need and long to do so. It is easy to bore our friends by reciting our own problems incessantly. Friendships must involve give and take in equal proportions. We have to be willing to share a friend's woes as well as seeking his sympathy for our own.

Making friends with others in need
Because we have experienced the pangs of loneliness we are able more fully to feel compassion for others in need; the depressed, the bereaved, the mentally and physically handicapped, the very old, those in hospital or with marriage or family problems. It may be possible to find ways of helping them, and this, in turn, will help us in our own loneliness.

Many libraries have schemes for taking books to the housebound, some local councils run voluntary services, the W.R.V.S are always looking for volunteers and the Samaritans are glad of sympathethic people to act as telephone contacts. There are countless elderly folk in homes or hospitals who are desperately lonely and a letter to the matron is all that is required to discover if she has any such who would welcome a visitor. The vicar or priest of the local church would be in touch with others needing friendship and help, and church social groups for all ages often exist where we would be likely to find people needing companionship. To satisfy the needs of our fellows is the surest way of defeating loneliness in ourselves. Dale Carnegie summed it up in these words: "You can make more friends in two months by becoming interested in other people that you can make in two years by trying to get other people interested in you."

Taking up a cause

Libraries and sometimes local newspapers keep lists of the various charities, self-help groups and associations operating in their area, with names and addresses of their secretaries. One good way of breaking out of the prison of loneliness is becoming absorbed in helping a cause which we feel to be worthy of assistance. Animal and children's charities are always popular, but old people's welfare groups and the many disablement associations are equally deserving. There are sometimes environmental bodies, neighbourhood councils, or political groups in the region, all of which would welcome help, and to serve in a charity shop is a wonderful way of meeting and talking to many people.

The best approach is to select a cause, then contact the person in charge to ask what assistance is required. Even if it is only to take a collecting tin on a Flag Day, this is an excellent way of meeting others. In the event of the charity having little to offer we can easily try another. Help is always needed somewhere and we are then in touch with fellow-helpers whose interests match our own.

Once we have begun to look outside ourselves, new doors will open and new opportunities present themselves. To run a money-raising event, for example, is not nearly as daunting as it sounds, and something like a Coffee Morning, if held on a small scale, can be attempted almost single-handed. It needs a little advertisement; cards in nearby shops or notes through neighbours' doors, perhaps, offering a Bring and Buy stall, so that other saleable goods are brought in, and possibly a raffle. All that is required is a few goods to sell, some prizes and tickets for the raffle if this is to be included, and the provision of coffee and a biscuit at a reasonable price for all who attend. The charity to be aided by this effort should be approached beforehand, so that fellow-supporters may also attend and perhaps offer material help, such as providing home-made cakes which always sell well at this sort of function.

Running a jumble sale stall can be surprisingly enjoyable. All sorts of treasures are unearthed, and the hurly-burly of the sale itself soon dispels any sense of loneliness or boredom. These sales require men as well as women; a doorman, a cashier, strong arms to shift the heavier items, dealing with second-hand books and bric-a-brac, and drivers to collect donated goods; all these tasks await the willing volunteer.

The W.R.V.S often require male helpers to drive their Meals on Wheels vans, assist with heavy lifting and to visit some of their invalid men clients. Once we have become really involved with a cause that is worth supporting, we will feel that our lives have purpose, and loneliness will be relegated to the past.

Making friends with life

Life is a truly wonderful gift. A stone or a mountain is part of the universe, yet completely unaware of it. We, through our senses of sight, hearing, touch, taste, and smell can appreciate all the qualities of the world we live in and the amazing, incomprehensible miracle of life itself. It is sad that the sense of wonder which all children possess is so easily lost and that we, as adults, take entirely for granted the stars, the soap bubble, the acorn, the clouds, the mountain peaks, the butterfly and all the myriad beauties which surround us.

When we consider that life has been gradually evolving over countless millions of years, that our own time on earth is likely to span only seven decades, that for all our accumulated knowledge we understand so little of the mystery of our being, it seems incredible that so often we become bored with the passing days, wishing our life away and seeing no purpose in it. When we are lonely we tend to live inside ourselves, cutting ourselves off from the world about us. The way of hope is to emerge from this shell and begin to discover life again and to rejoice in it.

The first step may be to venture into our local environment, to explore parks and interesting buildings, take short bus or train trips and reconnoitre new areas and neighbouring towns. Coach excursions make it simple to travel further afield to places of interest, to view stately homes or investigate historical sites. Coach travel is preferable to driving alone by car, for on such trips other single people who may be looking for companionship will frequently be met. We need to be bold enough to set off on holiday alone. Even if we do not make new friends in the course of it, it is infinitely preferable to staying isolated at home, and we learn more about this earth we inhabit, whether we holiday abroad or merely in a neighbouring town.

All through our lives we are gathering knowledge and continually making fresh discoveries. Education does not cease when we leave school, and the more we learn the more interesting life becomes, and the more our own personalities will develop. Reading opens the door to new aspects of life. We have only to visit a library to find adequate supplies of books which introduce us to the riches of philosophy, religion or history, provide an insight into the lives of the famous, or stimulate our imagination with stories of mystery, romance or scientific speculation into the future.

Music, poetry and art offer us still further avenues of exploration. We can either enjoy them as an audience will, listening, reading and appreciating these skills, or we can try for ourselves to partake of them, learning to play an instrument, paint a picture or compose lines of verse. These are creative and deeply satisfying activities, bringing their own rich rewards and greatly increasing our enjoyment of life. The world of sport also points a way of escape from lonely isolation, again providing opportunities to watch or to participate, and to do either will bring us into the company of others of a like mind.

"Life is for living", wrote the poet Rilke, and, centuries before his time, St. Paul said, "I have learned, in whatsoever state I am, therewith to be content." So let us try to love life, to be grateful for it, and to appreciate it as fully as we can.

And, finally, we must never feel sorry for ourselves
How easy it is when we are lonely to pity ourselves, to feel that we are the victims of a cruel fate and that, somehow, the rest of the world is at fault for neglecting us. Loneliness is an attitude of mind which is very hard to alter. It becomes a habit and a pattern from which we must make every effort to free ourselves. This does require courage. It is simpler to nurse feelings of self-pity, not to risk making overtures of friendship for fear of rebuff, and keep to the old familiar routine. We must be willing to change our outlook on life and begin new ventures. It can be done, however old we are; however long we have been shut into the prison of isolation. We have to train ourselves to think positively, to look for the good things of life, and to seek out others, not for what they may give to us, but for what we may offer them.

These, then, are the ways out of loneliness along which hope will guide us. Following such paths we will be able to exchange that loneliness for solitude, and, as we become courageous enough to reach out to others, the terrifying sense of isolation will slowly fade until it has disappeared completely from our lives.

2. I Can't Get Over my Bereavement

The death of someone we love, even when a terminal illness has prepared us for the inevitable outcome, must always be a grievous blow, and to many a terrible and heart-rending sorrow, inflicting a wound so deep that we feel it can never be healed. Glib platitudes from well-meaning friends are useless. The pain is too real to be dismissed with an easy 'Time is a great healer; you'll get over it eventually.' We don't get over it. Such a traumatic event must bring about changes within ourselves and life can never again be as it was before. A tree that loses a main limb in a storm does not die but henceforth its growth will change. Sometimes it will produce stronger roots to compensate, or it may lean to one side because its balanced shape is lost. Yet it will continue its life as a tree. So it is with us when we suffer bereavement. We have to learn to live again but in a different way.

The pain of a bereavement is bound to affect us profoundly; the greater the love we have shared, the deeper will be the heartache when we are left alone. A time of mourning has to be endured, and, indeed, it is harmful for us to supress our symptoms of grief in order to present a brave face to the world. We have to go through this stage of desolation and sorrow. Yet it should not lead us to despair. Changed though life perforce must be, we have eventually to take it up again with courage and determination. We need to learn how to continue the rest of life's journey alone.

There will come a time when we feel within ourselves

that the period of mourning should end and we should try
to go forward. It is, perhaps, the hardest decision we will
ever have to make, this resolution to go on living again
keeping hold of hope, even though, for a while, it will be
like walking in the darkness without aim or purpose. It
takes great courage, but it can and must be done. So, when
despair sweeps over us, we need to look at the ways in
which hope can help us to endure.

First, let us assess our own attitude to death. When we
are young we tend to think of it as an outrage, an un-
thinkable obscenity and the ultimate evil. As we grow
older, we begin to see that death is a necessary part of life.
As we are born, go through childhood, adolescence,
maturity and old age, so we will die in the natural order
of things. Our bodies are designed to serve us for a limited
period only, just as any machine will need replacement
after prolonged use. We begin to understand that death is
unavoidable and that life, such as we know it on earth,
must have a limited span. But premature death of babies,
children or young people is harder to accept. Why must
this be?

We have to consider now whether we believe that our
allotted time on earth is all that we have, or whether, in
some way, life will continue beyond death, or even existed
before our birth. If life is limited to this earth, it is surely
utterly pointless and a cruel mockery. If being on earth is
merely endlessly to propagate more life, born only to even-
tual annihilation, why should the life-force be so powerful
and so indomitably persistent? It would have no motivation for such tenacity of purpose. St. Paul said, "If in this
life only we have hope in Christ, we are of all men most
miserable".

To me it seems more reasonable to believe that in some
way life must go on, that only the body dies and that we
ourselves continue our journey, taking with us all that we
have learned in the course of our passage through a human
experience. "Death", wrote Rabindranath Tagore, "is not
extinguishing the Light – but putting out the light because

Dawn has come." If we believe then that all life is in God's hands, even the death of a child does not appear as an irremediable tragedy. Robert Browning compared God to a potter designing beautiful vases. If one was spoiled in the process, He took the same clay and remoulded it to a more perfect shape. His poem concludes:

> Maker, remake, complete;
> I trust what Thou shalt do.

So, in death, we do not slip from His hands, but our lives, however briefly lived on this earth, have needed that birth and coming into being and will continue to develop under His care. It is only our conception of the finality of death which causes us to view it with such horror and despair.

To believe that those who have died have merely gone ahead of us, not even very far from where we are, and that we shall eventually be re-united with them is a very real hope and held by too many to be simply wishful thinking. We cannot, of course, have infallible proof, but we do have very good grounds for such a belief. Many have felt, in a most positive way, the presence of those who have died; not in the sense of a ghostly or supernatural appearance, but just as a quiet assurance that all is well with them. I have experienced this myself. That Jesus was seen by His friends, spoke to them and remained with them for some weeks after His death is not easy to explain away, and I believe it to be true.

So, in this hope, we can be comforted by some words on death written by Canon Scott Holland:

> Death is nothing at all . . . . . I have slipped away into the next room. I am I and you are you. Whatever we were to each other that we are still. Call me by my old familiar name, speak to me in the easy way which you always used. Put no difference in your tone; wear no forced air of solemnity or sorrow. Laugh as we always laughed at the little jokes we enjoyed together. Play,

smile, think of me, pray for me. Let my name be ever
the household word it always was. Let it be spoken
without effort, without the ghost of a shadow on it.
Life means all that it ever meant. It is the same as it
ever was; there is absolutely unbroken continuity.
What is this death but a negligible accident? Why
should I be out of mind because I am out of sight? I
am waiting for you for an interval, somewhere very
near, just around the corner. All is well.

Next, we must remember that to continue to mourn for
the ones who have died for the rest of our lives would
surely not be their wish. They would not want us to be
unhappy. So, for their sakes, we should try to take up the
threads of life again and seek to live in the way they would
desire. To laugh, to go out and about and enjoy life once
more in no way implies disrespect to the dead; in fact
many in their lifetime are concerned lest their death will
bring unhappiness to those for whom they care the most.
They would naturally wish to remain in our memory, but
not that that memory should bring sorrow. It is good to
recall happiness of days gone by and to feel gratitude for
it, but we should certainly continue to love those who have
died, to pray for them, and to hold them in our present
thoughts; not thinking of their lives as belonging only to
the past. Love is eternal, for religion teaches us that love
is God, and God is love. Love cannot die, and if we love
deeply then that love is a strong bond holding us together
– whether living or dead is immaterial. As Edith Sitwell
wrote:

> Love is not lost by death –
> Nothing is lost, as all in
> the end is harvested.

Thus, as we prepare to go on with the business of living,
hope tells us that we are not utterly alone; we are not
wholly separated from those we have lost; they still care

for us as we for them, and as we believe in God's love and protection, so we may be sure that their love is still with us.

Despite this reassurance, to contemplate a new future after suffering bereavement is as much a major hurdle as starting our career, or changing to an entirely new type of employment. New routines must be learned, and to those who for many years have lived in close partnership, each coping with a different side of domestic life, the transition can be hard indeed. Husbands must now undertake cooking, washing and cleaning; wives deal with home maintainance and financial matters. These basic skills are necessary for survival and, just by demanding our attention, can divert our minds to some extent from our sense of wretchedness and isolation. We do need to occupy our time as much as possible, and even if the inclination is not there, to seek the company of others. Associations such as CRUSE, for widows and widowers, can supply valuable support here. It is hope that will give us courage as we struggle to build up again our broken lives. Let us think of death without shrinking, seeing it hopefully, with clearer eyes and confident hearts, as did an anonymous American poet who wrote:

> I have seen death too often to believe in death.
> It is not an ending, but a withdrawal,
> As one who finishes a long journey,
> Stills the motors,
> Turns off the lights,
> Steps from his car,
> And walks up the path
> To the home that awaits him.

It takes much fortitude to begin to look into the future and see there something other than black despair. There will be decisions to make and we must be wary of making radical changes without due consideration and care. We feel, perhaps, the urge to move to a new location to escape the many sad associations which the family home now holds.

Yet, when the initial shock is over and our grief less poignant, we may find those familiar surroundings comforting and be grateful that they bring back memories of shared happiness. We also have to take into account that we will be leaving behind friends, acquaintances, and accustomed and well-loved haunts, if we plan to begin anew in an unknown neighbourhood. Similarly, although for many it will be out of the question, the possibility of re-marriage may occur to us. Here again, this is not a decision to be made in haste. It may, indeed, be the right step to take, but to re-marry merely to escape from loneliness is a recipe for disaster. We must give ourselves time to plan for the future, considering all the options we have; new doors will open as we begin to go forward and slowly our lives will re-shape themselves into a changed pattern.

Our mourning for those we have lost is an expression of our love for them. We can equally use that love by going hopefully into the unknown future, living each day as well and as bravely as we are able for their sake. The saying, "there is a past which is gone for ever, but there is a future which is still our own" is not an expression of nostalgia for the past, but a signpost to urge us to go forward on the journey of life, not forgetting the past, but living more courageously in the future because of it. And this is the way of hope.

3. My Life is so Useless and Dreary

Tennyson's Mariana echoes these despondent
words:

> . . . . . 'My life is dreary,'
> She said, 'I am aweary, aweary.
> I would that I were dead!'

If we honestly believe that our existence has no meaning
or purpose, if nothing we experience gives us any pleasure
or satisfaction, our condition must indeed be dreary, futile
and hopeless. We have been thinking of life as a journey,
and on any journey there will be stretches of the road that
are dull and uninteresting. In such circumstances we will
trudge along seeing little to stimulate us, but knowing that
before long the scenery will change and that, possibly just
around the next corner, we shall glimpse mountain peaks,
alluring woodland glades, or green meadows studded with
summer flowers. The constantly varying landscape will
make the journey less wearisome, and unexpected revela-
tions of beauty, however brief, bring cheer to weary
hearts. Sometimes deserts or barren plains can extend for
many miles, but sooner or later they must end. All we have
to do is to keep walking. To sit by the roadside is pointless
– there is no choice but to plod on. The sensible traveller
well find ways of relieving the tedium; he will fill his mind
with cheerful thoughts, whistle, sing, speculate on what
he will find at his journey's end, and plan hopefully for the
future. If his surroundings hold nothing of interest, he will
lift his thoughts to pleasanter considerations.

So it is with life. We cannot always live in a state of ecstatic bliss; these moments are rare and to be treasured; most of life will be humdrum and pedestrian and there will also be periods when the sheer monotony of our daily routine will weary us. That is when we must take steps to ameliorate such fatigue and boredom.

First, we need to consider this sense of being useless. It is an absolute fallacy. No living thing is or can be useless, for nothing can be more purposeful and charged with potential being than the life-force which permeates it. It is this vital energy which causes heavy paving stones to be pushed up by the thrusting roots of trees and shrubs, enables frail plants to grow and flourish in mere traces of rubble in wall crevices, and, when rain brings the conditions needed for their growth, brings into bourgeoning leaf and flower seeds which have lain dormant for years in sand and dried out river beds. How rightly we assert, "Where there is life there is hope".

Yet there are many who, looking around them, feel inadequate and inferior compared to their fellows. They see themselves as being as insignificant as a single grain of sand on the seashore or a blade of grass in a meadow, too minute to be of any account in the vastness of time and space. But we must reflect that everything is made up of very small components. All matter consists of atoms; our entire electoral system is determined by single votes. We may still be inclined to feel that, even so, the individual will be merged into the whole and lost. But this is not so. In fact, it is the other way round; a vast and complicated machine will break down if there is a fault in its smallest cog. The effect which we as individuals have on those around us is as far-reaching as ripples from a stone thrown into the centre of a pond, which will go on widening until they reach its furthest bounds.

Everyone matters; no-one is inferior to his neighbour. A jigsaw puzzle is ruined if one small piece is lost. Each part, however humble, is necessary for the whole to be complete and we all have a unique place to fill; the characteristics we have and the talents we possess qualifying us, and no other, to occupy that position. It is more pleasing to listen to a choir singing in harmony than to a single voice or to all in unison. Who are we to question the value of the part we take? If the quality of our lives does not resemble that of our neighbours we should not assume that we are of less value than they. We all blend into the whole, and all contribute to the complex pattern of the universe.

And if we fail and do not fulfil that purpose? Will the universe in consequence suffer? I think not. As in the operation of any complicated machinery, adjustments and amendments must constantly be made. We have been given free-will; we have the option to bring to fruition or to deny the potential which is in us. But we are surely the losers if we remain passive and, as the Biblical parable succinctly expresses it, bury our one talent in the ground. The necessary duties will be carried out, if not by us then by others, but what a waste it will be if we choose to leave undone those responsibilities which have been designated to us. True happiness, I am convinced, lies in discovering our own particular niche, small though it may be, and occupying it to the best of our ability. It seems reasonable to suppose that to fail in this might necessitate being born again, returning to the starting point, being, in fact, barred from making any further progress on our journey until we have learned and understood the purpose of our existence here on earth.

What we have to do, therefore, is to re-assess the valuation we are putting on our lives, recognise the talents and abilities which we certainly possess and begin to use them more fully to the advantage both of ourselves and others. It has been wisely said,

> Life without purpose
> Is barren indeed;
> There can't be a harvest
> Unless we plant seed.

To set about planting that seed, in hopeful expectation of

its growth, is what we must endeavour to do and these are the steps to follow:

We begin by drawing up three lists:

LIST ONE   Write down all the things that you are able to do. Do not dismiss this by saying, 'But I can't do anything'. That means you are mentally adding the word 'worthwhile'. Whether you think they are important of not, write them down. The list will be a long one. Everyone, unless physically handicapped, can begin with, I can see, hear, smell, taste and touch. These are common to all of us, but are the basis of all our skills. To these you will probably add walk, talk, run, read, write, eat and drink. Because you can think, learn and understand, three more vital assets, you are able to read newspapers and watch the television, thus increasing your comprehension of the world, its problems and its politics. Through books or by travel you can also find out about other countries and their peoples, about plants, animals, birds and the countryside, and the history of our own and distant lands. Knowledge opens countless doors.

   Think of all that you achieve by using your hands, and do not be afraid of putting down really elementary accomplishments. For example:
You may not be a Cordon Bleu cook, but you can boil potatoes or an egg.
Designing a dress may be beyond you, but you can sew on a button.
If you have never learned to drive a car, you can still push a pram or a wheel-chair, or, maybe, ride a bicycle.
You can write a letter, even if you do not aspire to the authorship of a book.
You are able to appreciate music by listening to the radio or a cassette, without having the skill to play an instrument.
You may be hopeless at painting flowers, but you can arrange a few in a pleasing manner in a vase.
Write down all these things and more. They are only

modest achievements, but by mastering them, and, through practice, improving on them, you will find it easier to attempt more ambitious undertakings.

LIST TWO   This will be shorter, but is equally important. Write down on this list anything you can do which not everyone else can aspire to. It may include knitting, embroidery, painting the house, making a cake, driving a car, bathing a baby, doing a crossword puzzle, swimming, etc. etc. It will still record quite simple tasks such as telling the time, making a bed, scrambling eggs, mending a fuse, changing a light bulb, or using a laundrette. There are many who have not learned to do these things. Carry on with this list until you have made it as long and as comprehensive as possible.

LIST THREE   Now you must write down those things you have always wanted to do, whether or not you think you are capable of them.

Having made the three lists, read them through carefully. You will probably be surprised at how versatile you already are. Then re-consider list three. There is no reason at all why you should not achieve some of these aims. You will have to be prepared to work hard and to persevere. Determination and hope together make a very good partnership. Of course, some ambitions must remain dreams. We cannot, at the age of 40, expect to become a ballerina, or at 60 and with no previous experience of mountaineering, climb the Matterhorn. On the other hand, I recently read in the national press of a 90 year old who has written a book, a man of 86 who took and passed an "O" level examination, and a disabled lone yachtsman who made a successful 74 day crossing to the Azores and back to Penzance. Fewer things than we suppose are actually impossible.

The best way to proceed is to look at list two, the skills you already possess, and decide which of those will best fit you to tackle some project in list three. Think about it carefully, and work out what you need to do; perhaps attend evening classes, obtain study books from the library, join a club or association where you will meet people with a similar interest, practise for a set period each day, and so on. Planting seed takes effort, but it is always worth the trouble.

When we feel useless, we are imposing limitations on ourselves, building unnecessary walls which shut us in and stifle our ambition. We have to break down these walls and refuse to let them imprison us. Physically handicapped people often surprise us by their cheerfulness and inventiveness. They are prohibited from much which we simply take for granted; they respond by offering their courage and their good spirits as a positive contribution to life, so that others will be cheered by their example. Such lives may be restricted, but are never useless or dreary. Limitations can always be overcome. Richard Lovelace wrote:

> Stone walls do not a prison make,
> Nor iron bars a cage.

In these days of mass production many must necessarily be employed in dull and repetitive work; it does not follow that our whole lives must be set in the same monotonous mould, nor should such work be considered useless. We depend for our comforts and well-being on the labours of countless unknown people, and others are benefitted in turn from the work we do. It may be unexciting, but it should not restrict us in any real sense from enjoying a fulfilled and contented existence. Our minds are unfettered, our thoughts our own, our brains alert to serve us, and there will be ample free time to spend as the inclination takes us.

All that is needful is the will be go forward boldly along new and unexplored paths, discovering as we do so the whole range of our abilities. It has been truly said that we must not rest in our limitations, but rather make use of our opportunities, or, in the more picturesque words of an ancient Chinese proverb:

We cannot prevent the birds of sadness from flying over our heads – but we can prevent them building nests in our hair.

4. I'm Always Tense and Worried

It has been said that 'worry is moving into tomorrow ahead of schedule', and there are numerous proverbs to warn against jumping ditches or crossing bridges before we reach them. We recognise the wisdom of these words, but it is by no means easy to put them into practice. Worry cannot be turned off like a tap. If we are worriers by nature, then it is extremely difficult to set all anxiety aside, calm our minds and live serene and untroubled lives.

It is only natural that caring parents should be concerned for the welfare of their children, and children for parents, feeling disquiet when they are ill or exposed to danger. If we love others we cannot avoid being anxious on their behalf. It is when worry moves from the present into the future, anticipating trouble and ill fortune; when it establishes itself as a habit of mind, that it becomes, at best useless and a waste of time, and at worst can seriously damage our health. Although to live one day at a time is, generally speaking, good advice, we cannot, of course, avoid planning ahead to some extent. Forethought, however, is very different from anxious thought.

It is the constant foreboding about what might happen, the nagging 'what ifs......?' going round and round in our brains which are so harmful. Worry causes tensions to build up and we find that we are restless, edgy, and unable to sleep or to concentrate. Tension in itself and in the short term does no damage; in fact it gives us extra energy to deal with a crisis, work longer hours, or carry out some difficult task requiring all our concentration. But it is not a state to be maintained continuously. If we consider a child's balloon we can see that it needs to be inflated only to a limited degree. Under-inflation will leave it wrinkled and too heavy to float easily, correctly filled it will be light and buoyant, yet able to withstand a reasonable amount of handling, but too much air will cause the rubber to be too thinly stretched, so that it bursts at the slightest knock. Similarly, prolonged tension puts a strain on the body and can bring on headaches, migraine, backache, indigestion and other unpleasant symptoms. These are warning signals that we are coming excessively under stress and must try to unwind.

Sometimes the nature of our employment is stress-inducing. To work for long periods in the midst of clamour and turmoil, racing to meet deadlines, burdened with responsibilities and ever increasing pressures is to make impossible demands on ourselves. The human body is resilient but not indestructible.

We cannot avoid stressful situations at times – they are part of life. But we have to allow ourselves periods of rest in which to slow down again. A car will stall if the engine is over-heated. To spur ourselves feverishly beyond our resources must inevitably bring about symptoms of strain. This urge to forge relentlessly on is not just a characteristic of the modern way of life; indeed we now have far more leisure time and freedom than many of our forebears. The opening words of the Desiderata, found in a church in Baltimore in 1692, are:

> Go placidly amid the noise and haste, and remember what peace there may be in silence.

Wise words then, and equally so now.

When worry, overwork or exhaustion have escalated into a state of tension we find the condition very hard to reverse. We feel that worrying has almost become an obligation, that to worry about a possible future mischance will somehow prevent it from occurring; a sort of insurance against disaster. Worries are poor bedfellows;

yet how frequently we lie awake hour after hour fretting about what may or may not happen the next day. We cannot let them go. And always we imagine that the very worst will come to pass. Worrying should be left to puppies; sadly is is all too often a human pastime.

By worrying we turn our backs on hope and look only at the negative side of life. We can see, when we think about it rationally, that worry will achieve nothing. We are told by doctors that prolonged worry can shorten lives, bringing on heart attacks, strokes, depression and, in some cases, even cancer. Yet, knowing this, we seem to be unable to escape from it. What is the remedy? We need to do two things; to ease the tension and to achieve peace of mind.

Easing Tension

We may not always realise how tense we are; it is sometimes easier to recognise the signs in other people. We notice that they are sitting uncomfortably on the extreme edge of a chair, with hunched shoulders and tightly clenched jaws. Perhaps they are screwing up their hands into fists, tapping their feet or biting their nails. Many people become restless, unable to sit still for a moment or, if they are holding anything, will twist it round and round in their fingers. We may be unaware that we are doing some of these things ourselves. Tense people are often heavy smokers, because holding a cigarette gives them something with which to occupy themselves; tension seems to require constant activity.

We must recognise, then, such signs of tension when they occur. Sometimes they will force themselves on our attention, when, for instance, we have a severe headache, or pains in the back, neck or shoulders. This discomfort is often the result of stiffening and tightening of the muscles, and to ease them we should try to relax our whole bodies. Relaxation does not come easily. It has to be worked at and achieved slowly.

The first and most obvious thing is to lessen the work load, take life at a slower pace and allow ourselves small breaks in the daily routine.

Next, half an hour each day should be set aside for relaxation exercises. We will need a quiet room where we can lie comfortably on a bed or on the floor. Each part of the body has to be relaxed in turn, beginning with the head and face and working downwards to the feet, tensing up the muscles as tightly as possible and then slowly allowing them to slacken, until finally the whole body is completely limp and unresisting, as though sinking into the depths of a soft cloud. Then we encourage the mind to relax by concentrating on something restful and pleasant; an image of the sea, perhaps, and unruffled lake, or a beautiful flower. Quiet background music sometimes helps to calm us. These times of stillness will gradually rest our tired minds, but it will take time and daily repetition.

Correct breathing is an important part of relaxation, and a few slow, deep breaths always have a quietening effect. If we have to cope with a stressful situation, to pause first and breathe slowly for a few moments will certainly help us to deal with the crisis. There are a number of very good cassettes on the markets which will give more detailed advice on breathing and relaxation exercises.

Peace of Mind

Deep peace, pure white of the moon to you;
Deep peace, pure green of the grass to you;
Deep peace, pure brown of the earth to you;
Deep peace, pure grey of the dew to you;
Deep peace, pure blue of the sky to you;
Deep peace of the running wave to you,
Deep peace of the flowing air to you,
Deep peace of the quiet earth to you.

Fiona Macleod

These lines, read slowly and thoughtfully, will often bring about a sense of calm when our minds are troubled.

We live in a world which is in a state of continual turmoil. Newspaper headlines scream at us of disasters, battles and violent crime, the threat of atomic warfare hangs over us, unemployment, rising costs, and mounting pressures and strains at work and at home crowd in on us daily, so that peace and tranquillity seem almost unattainable. To find peace of mind is a deep human need, and if we are to preserve our sanity and establish some order in our lives we must discover it. But how?

Let us look at nature. Much of our environment is artificial, and we can become stifled by the high-rise flats, the roar of machinery and traffic, and the fevered rush, bustle and noise of the town. We have to allow ourselves time to absorb the serenity of the earth, to feel the calm strength of the hills, the quiet influence of streams that have murmured gently over the same pebbles for centuries of time, the green restfulness of meadows and woods which cover so much of our beautiful countryside. W. B. Yeats, in his poem "The Lake Isle of Innisfree", spoke of his longing to escape to this lovely retreat where he could hear

Lake water lapping with low sounds by the shore.

Water always has a therapeutic influence on our minds, whether we are watching waves breaking effortlessly over the sand, listening to the foaming spray of a waterfall cascading down its rocky path, or looking at reflections cast by a lofty mountain on the placid surface of the lake at its foot. This is probably why fishing is recommended for those who need a rest cure. Hours spent quietly by a gently-flowing river bring healing and peace. A calm sea also conveys to us the same sense of tranquillity. Gulls float serenely on the purling tide, as Milton described so beautifully when he said, "birds of calm sit brooding on the charmèd wave". I can remember, many years ago, walking one summer evening by the Solway Firth, and seeing the setting sun throw a radiant crimson and gold pathway across its waters, the light of sea and air seeming to mingle together in a wonderful glow that spread across the land to our very feet. It was so quiet and still; as if the earth were resting for a while and relaxing after the day's labours.

Music can also bring peace to our minds, allowing us, as we listen to its gentle ministration, to unwind from the stresses and strains of the past. Sometimes we find peace by absorbing ourselves in a favourite hobby or creative work of art. But, even if we have no opportunity to seek the calm of the countryside or follow a leisure time pursuit, it is still possible to discover an inner peace within ourselves. Browning once wrote:

> There is an inmost centre in us all
> Where truth abides in fulness.

When we enter a church we feel instinctively the peace that fills it. The older the church the more profound is the atmosphere of calmness and tranquillity which enfolds us. Perhaps this is because of the many who have prayed there throughout the centuries. Within its walls we seem to hear the voice of Jesus, "Come unto me all ye that labour and are heavy laden, and I will give you rest". And we remember how He calmed the storm on Galilee and the fears of His disciples with the words, "Peace, be still". The Church has always taught the value of stilling our minds from the distractions of life so that we are able to draw closer to God. 'Retreats' are sometimes held, so that people may have the opportunity to meditate in a quiet place for a while.

Meditation is an essential part of most of the world's great religions, bringing, as it does, comfort and healing to the mind. In recent times Christianity seemed to lose sight of its importance, and many were driven to seek it outside the Church. The young turned eagerly to transcendental meditation and Yoga, finding in them the peace they so earnestly desired. It is encouraging that today many Christian people are re-discovering the value of both meditation and spiritual healing, making them an integral part of their worship.

Many centuries ago, Dame Julian of Norwich said this of peace:

> Thus I saw that God is our very Peace, and He is our sure Keeper when we are ourselves in unpeace, and He continually worketh to bring us into endless peace.

To so absorb peace into our lives will set us free from the heavy burden of strain and worry, enabling us to find once more hope and true joy in living.

5. I'm Afraid all the Time

Most of us can vividly recall our childhood fears; the faceless spectres that lurked in shadowy corners, dark cupboards, or under the bed waiting to seize us. Those games of never treading on a line for fear of being eaten by bears were only half make-believe and, when night time came, the terror was all too real. My own particular dread, at the age of about four, was of passing a drain at the back of the house. My imagination had conjured up two evil presences lying in wait for me there with the intention of dragging me into its murky depths. The fears of childhood are natural enough to understand. Children comprehend little of the nature of the world around them, and when confronted with a new experience they have no way of knowing the outcome. It is only when a familiar pattern is built up that confidence is recovered. This is why, when well-loved possessions and playthings are hidden by darkness, so many children need reassurance that their parents have not deserted them, that the accustomed everyday objects are still in their places, and that all is well. These childish fears are slowly outgrown, but they still remain in our memories.

The instinct of fear plays a necessary part in our lives. Without it we should be continually at risk, for the world holds many real dangers. We need to appreciate the potential hazards of fire, water, electricity, poisonous substances and plants, wild animals and heavy or fast-moving machinery. Fear will restrain us when we might otherwise take unnecessary risks. Its function is to act as a warning light, alerting us to danger, so that we may then assess the position and decide whether or not to take action. There is no shame at all in being afraid in times of danger. True heroes are not those who know no fear, but those who, despite it, will carry on with what they feel is right to do.

However, to live continually in subjection to fear is to be as a child peopling the darkness with monsters of his own fantasy. Fear should be a servant, not our master. If we find that it has taken us over and is dominating our lives we must try to discover why this should be, and how we can overcome it.

The first step is to face it. Here are two quotations:

> 1. like one that on a lonely road
>   doth walk in fear and dread,
>   and having once turned round, walks on
>   and turns no more his head;
>   because he knows a frightful fiend
>   doth close behind him tread.

> 2. Ye fearful saints, fresh courage take;
>   the clouds you so much dread
>   are big with mercy, and will break
>   in blessings on your head.

Had the traveller in the first verse really stopped and faced that fiend, he would have found it but a product of his own imagining. His first terrified glance had transformed a shadow into a dreadful, menacing evil, and so he walked on, tormented by his fear. The second verse also points out how unreasonable our fears can be. The very things that fill us with the most foreboding so often work out to our advantage.

Prolonged, nagging fear that becomes our daily companion is usually the fear of fear itself. This we must overcome because it is both unnecessary and harmful. It can build up into phobias which will impose so many limitations that our lives will become inhibited and stunted by

them. Let us, then, look at our fear, try to analyse it and
decide what it is that frightens us.

In some cases it can be guilt. There may be something
in the past, perhaps the very far distant past, done, or said,
or indeed not done, which is chafing us continually. We
may fear the consequences that it could bring, or regret the
harm caused. If we do regret it, then we are already half
way to recovery. We must go on to seek forgiveness, and
we need this in three ways; from the person or persons we
have wronged, from God, or if we have no belief in a
personal God, then from the condemnation of our own
conscience, and thirdly, we must be willing to forgive
ourselves, this being, perhaps, the hardest of all. If, having
expressed regret for a past wrong and done all we can in
reparation, the injured person is unwilling to forgive, or if
they have died and we are unable to tell them of our con-
trition, this is immaterial now. We cannot undo the past
and we have done all we can. God's forgiveness, if we are
truly repentant, is assured. We must then go on to accept
it, stop blaming ourselves, and realise that we are now able
to start again, freed from the burden of guilt.

Another very common reason for fear is a subconscious
memory of some trauma of childhood. This can be the
origin of various phobias which occur in adult life, and
sometimes to remember what triggered off that fear helps
to bring it back into proportion. A mother's terror of
thunderstorms, or her aversion to snakes will convey itself
to her family, even if she tries to conceal it.
Claustrophobia can develop if a small child is shut in a
dark room or cupboard, or even if, when being dressed, a
tight jersey becomes stuck over his head. For many years
I had the compulsion of needing to sleep with my back
against a wall. It was a long time before I discovered the
reason. When very young I had been taken to the cinema
and the film portrayed a sinister, hooded figure who crept
around at night stabbing people in the back. Presumably,
after this, I had felt safer if my back was protected by
the bedroom wall, and once I remembered the film and

realised the connection the phobia was no longer with me.

Fear may result from a lack of love and affection. The child crying out in the night for a drink of water is not so much thirsty as needing the assurance of his parents' presence and protection. However self-sufficient and independent we may feel ourselves to be, man is a gregarious animal and needs some contact with his kind. Even in adulthood we sometimes crave protection and consolation, though circumstances may decree that we must walk alone. The Bible speaks of the conies, small rabbit-like animals, and tells us that they are "a feeble folk, but they inhabit the rocks". They have the good sense to stay where they will find security and shelter. We, therefore, need our families and our friends, and if we are fearful of life, it will help us to seek companionship, even if only that of a cat or dog. If we believe in a caring God we have, like the conies, "the shadow of a great rock in a weary land". We can remember His promise to Joshua, "Be strong and of a good courage: be not afraid neither be thou dismayed; for the Lord thy God is with thee whithersoever thou goest". And, even more comforting, the words of Jesus to His disciples, "Lo, I am with you alway".

It may be that, having given careful thought to the problem, we can still find no explanation for our fears. In that case it is best, as far as we are able, to ignore them: we shall reach our destination despite them. It is encouraging to remember Christopher Columbus. He must have known fear, for in those days it was a common belief that to venture too far across the ocean was to incur a very real risk of falling from the edge of the world into an unfathomable abyss. And yet, when he set out on his famous voyage of discovery he didn't know where he was going. When he arrived on the strange shores of America, he didn't know where he was. When he got back he didn't even know where he had been. But he knew that, in the face of doubts and fears, he had carried on and he had found a great new world.

When I left school, I remember very clearly how apprehensive I was as I set out alone to embark on my first day at work. I was crossing Kew Bridge when, on the far side of the river, I noticed a large sign over a brewery. 'COURAGE' it said. So, taking fresh heart, I went on and discovered that I was able to cope, after all, with everything that was required of me.

It is not easy to push fears aside; we have to escape from them gradually. Some years ago I lived in the country, nearly two miles from the nearest bus stop. On dark, stormy nights it was quite hazardous to walk home, avoiding passing traffic, along the unlit country lanes which had many blind corners. I came to recognise some of the trees along the route, particularly one, a large spreading oak, which I called in my mind 'the safety tree', because once past it the road straightened out, and I was able to see the welcoming lights of the village in the distance. Reaching 'the safety tree' did not mean that I was at my journey's end, but it did mark the final stage on the road and encouraged me to go on. So, when we are fighting our fears, it helps to look for things throughout the day which are safe and reassuring and are, in effect, our 'safety trees'. They may be the comfort of a meal, half an hour with a book, a rest by the fire or the visit of a friend. If we are prepared to fight our fears little by little we will find them slowly melting away.

Finally, a very good weapon against fear is to develop a sense of humour. When I look back over the war years I can see how essential this was in keeping up the spirits of a nation living under constant threat of danger, both by day and night. The cartoonists came into their own, cheerful posters appeared everywhere, theatres and concert halls put on comedy shows, and the wry comments of 'Chad' looking over his wall were widely appreciated. When the V1 flying bombs were terrorising London, it was difficult to carry out a normal day's work. Eventually, in the office where I was employed, it was agreed that we should not go to the air-raid shelters each time the siren sounded; the alarms were so frequent that this would have rendered working impossible. Instead, if danger seemed imminent, we would dive under the heavy tables which at that time served us as desks. I can remember seeing the funny side of this on one occasion, as we all crouched there among the waste-paper bins, dignified bosses and humble clerks alike, for all the world like children playing hide and seek. Thoughts like these distracted our thoughts from the bombs whistling down and shattering buildings in the vicinity.

> Give to the winds thy fears;
> Hope and be undismayed.

These are lines from a popular hymn and advice worth following. We may expect the worst to happen, yet it seldom does. Let us, instead, travel on hopefully, putting determinedly aside that burden of unnecessary fear and anxiety.

6. I Feel Perpetually Tired

> Don't weep for me now,
> Don't weep for me never —
> I'm going to do nothing
> For ever and ever.

This inscription purportedly appeared on the tombstone of an overworked and downtrodden charwoman. Her words would surely find an echo in the heart of many a harrassed mother struggling to bring up a young family unaided. Life can sometimes lay heavy burdens on us and the way can be weary indeed. All the same, we cannot continue indefinitely in such a state of lassitude. Fatigue will slow us down progressively to the point of complete collapse, and we must find relief if ordinary tiredness has built up into a state of perpetual exhaustion.

It is natural, and indeed healthy, to feel tired at the close of day when our duties and labours are over. Then a few hours of leisure and a good night's rest will be all that is required to refresh and invigorate us to cope with the challenge of the new day. But something is obviously wrong if we are unable to relax, sleep fitfully and find ourselves just as tired when we awake.

Many factors have to be taken into account, but overwork or prolonged strain and worry are the most likely causes of persistent tiredness. It is not always easy, however, to alter such a situation. We may be caring for a sick or aged relative, struggling to keep a small business on its feet, coping with family problems, or trying to hold down a demanding job as well as bringing up children and running the home. Some people can take these complications in their stride; others can manage to carry on for quite a long period, but will eventually become worn out and exhausted.

It is essential, then, for some relief to be found, and aid is usually available if we know where to look for it. The doctor or social worker will advise on help for dependent or sick relatives, and there is a charity, The Association of Carers, who do useful work in this field. Sometimes convalescent or nursing homes will take patients for just a week or so, in order to give those who are caring for them a much-needed break. The social services can offer a great deal of assistance, either arranging visits from a nurse, supplying orthopaedic or incontinence aids, or arranging for Home Helps to take some of the load. Many towns have voluntary services which provide visitors, transport for journeys to and from hospital, or hot meals. Libraries keep records of self-help groups in the area which might be able to meet a specific need. The Citizens Advice Bureau is also a wonderful source of help for worries of any sort, and for more intimate family problems the Marriage Guidance Council will give friendly and confidential advice.

We have to be realistic about the amount of work we do, asking ourselves whether we are, perhaps, fixing standards that are unattainable. It is not imperative for the house to be cleaned from top to bottom daily. Children are far happier romping around on shabby furniture rather than being afraid to move for fear of disturbing a cushion. If we allow ourselves to become overtired, we are either tense and edgy, or listless and dull; poor company for the rest of the family, and certainly not finding any pleasure in life ourselves. So, if possible, the amount of daily work should be reduced.

We need to have definite periods each day which can be set apart for relaxation. Factories and offices know the value of tea-breaks; without them energy would flag and output suffer. Modern farming has changed out of all recognition in recent years, but in times past, a field lying fallow was a common sight. Before the days of chemical fertilisers it was usual to rotate the crops, because if a field grew root crops year after year, the soil would become impoverished as the plants absorbed the nourishment they required for growth. Poor and exhausted earth could be restored to fertility be leaving the field fallow for a year. This did not mean that the ground would stagnate and become infested with weeds. The farmer would plough it up first, then the soil would be left free to gather renewal from air, rain, sunshine and the chemical elements in the earth. Its reserves would be built up, so that when seeds were sown again the following year, a good crop would result. I sometimes think that fatigue develops as a result of continually using our reserves of energy and brain-power, giving them no renewal time; no time to lie fallow. If, therefore, we have been trying to carry too great a work load, some of the less essential tasks must be shed. It may even mean considering a part instead of full time job, for it is no exaggeration that people can literally work themselves to death. Surely in few cases can there be any justification for this. We know that in centuries past the life expectancy of child and adult workers in factories and mills was pitifully short. It is no advantage to make a little extra money at the expense of ruining our health.

We all need breaks in our everyday working lives; times to renew our spirits and build up our energy. To plod on with nothing to look forward to can only produce weariness and boredom.

Let us imagine a lone sailor struggling in the darkness to keep his little ship afloat while terrible storms rage around him. The ship is damaged and in danger of sinking, the storm grows worse and thunder crashes overhead. How thankful he will be if a flash of lightning reveals the safe, smooth beach of an island just ahead; how overjoyed to be able to land unharmed on the shore, and know that he has found shelter and deliverance in his time of need. When the tempest dies away and he is able to explore the island

and discover there green, shady woods, beautiful fruits and flowers, and fresh streams of water, he will feel himself to be in paradise. The poet Shelley once described life as a journey through perilous, stormy seas, but now and again, he said, we discover pleasant green isles and the joys of these make our weary travelling bearable and worthwhile. He wrote:

Many a green isle needs must be
In the deep wide sea of misery
Or the mariner, worn and wan
Never thus could voyage on,
Day and night and night and day,
Drifting on his dreary way
With the solid darkness black
Closing round his vessel's track,
And its ancient pilot, 'Pain'
Sits beside the helm again.

Green islands are our times of relaxation and pleasure, holidays, or escape from the tedious daily routine. They may be all that we need to overcome that besetting tiredness which can make life seem nothing but drudgery.

However, overwork is not the only reason for excessive fatigue. If no obvious answer can be found a doctor should be consulted, for it is a symptom of many illnesses, anaemia or depression for instance. Should a medical disorder be diagnosed, quite simple treatment may be all that is required to restore normal vitality.

A faulty diet can certainly be responsible for feelings of debility. Some protein foods – for example eggs, meat, cheese or fish – should be taken daily. Protein is also found in milk, nuts and pulses, and these should therefore be included in a vegetarian diet. Vitamin B, which is contained in wholemeal flour, is another good provider of energy.

Working in a stuffy or smoke-laden atmosphere is tiring. Our bodies need fresh air, sunlight and exercise, and will benefit from as much time as possible spent out of doors.

Much tiredness is mental rather than physical, so playing an energetic game or going for a brisk walk will often disperse the feeling of lethargy.

If you wake up feeling tired, it may be that you have got into a habit of not sleeping soundly. It is a great help to try to do something relaxing before going to bed, such as taking a short walk, or doing something divesting, so that you don't take worries to bed with you.

Boredom is another producer of fatigue. We need to have purpose in our lives to give them motivation, and if we drift aimlessly with no incentive to achieve anything, there is nothing to spur us on or encourage us to make any effort. We will inevitably become listless and lacking in energy.

Tired minds need vision. We have to be lifted out of the trite and commonplace, by realising the wonder and the miracle of this state of being which we call life; perhaps by catching a glimpse of the stars on a frosty night, as did Gerard Manley Hopkins when he wrote:

> Look at the stars! look, look up at the skies!
> O look at all the fire-folk sitting in the air!
> The bright boroughs, the circle-citadels there!

Then we can shake off the shackles of our drooping and hopeless thoughts and feel the ability once more to, 'mount up with wings as eagles; to run and not be weary; to walk and not faint'.

7.   People Always Seem to Put me Down

"They say. . . . . . . .What say they? Let them say." My mother would quote this when, as children, we were upset by adverse criticisms. I must admit, I never thought it particularly consoling. Our friends' and neighbours' opinions do matter to us; to be approved of and accepted as a member of society is a natural enough aspiration. It is only when the desire for popularity gets out of hand that problems can arise. We may destroy potential friendships by clinging too closely, being afraid to voice our own opinions, or by trying to mould our lives on those of others. Keeping up with the Joneses is a futile exercise, satisfying neither the Joneses nor ourselves.

The root of the trouble is a sense of inferiority and lack of self-confidence. Children whose parents are never satisfied with their achievements, belittle or, worse still, ridicule all that they do, will become timid, unaspiring adults, with little ambition or belief in their own ability. As a teacher I was often saddened when a small child, having struggled laboriously all the afternoon to complete some piece of handwork, would say to me, "It's no use my taking it home. Mummy would only throw it away". Children, and indeed adults, need some praise and encouragement along the way; continual criticism destroys confidence.

The pupils of the school I attended when I was young were divided into four teams; or houses as we called them, each with the name of a tree; beeches, chestnuts, elms and oaks. By good work or conduct we could win marks for our house; bad conduct meant that marks were deducted. Lost marks had to be reported, in person, to the house captain, a member of the sixth form, and this, in itself, was quite a deterrent. Order marks for bad conduct meant a loss of two marks, but if we then behaved impeccably for a further three weeks the two lost marks might be redeemed. Bad school work, however, could result in a 'rejected', entailing a loss of three marks and, unlike an order mark, was irredeemable. I always felt that there was some injustice here. We can, after all, control our behaviour to some extent, but if we happen to be inept at one particular subject no amount of conscientious study makes us brilliant in that field. My weakness was, and still is, mathematics. I seemed to have a mental block when the maths mistress was explaining the mysteries of logarithms, stocks and shares and so on. Consequently, I frequently had poor marks even for my most laboured efforts, and was once given a 'rejected' by a tutor whose patience was exhausted. I can still remember how devastated I felt. I had spent hours struggling with my homework. I really had done my best, and then had lost, irretrievably, three points for my house.

Rejection like this, whether of our work or ourselves, is always hurtful, and it is easy for us to label ourselves 'I'm a failure'. We feel that we have fallen short of our own and everyone else's expectations, and we blame ourselves for having done so. Yet, so often, what appears to be failure is nothing of the kind, and even genuine failure need not be a disaster and can be turned to good account. Let us consider what we mean by this word failure. No human being can succeed in everything, but all, in the course of their lives succeed in many things. We tend to take for granted the hundreds of skills which we possess. A young baby cannot control its body in any way; it has to learn to talk, walk, feed itself, dress itself, and later, at school age, to count and understand numbers, to read and to write. In all these processes it fails in its early attempts. We learn by trial an error; by failing and then trying again until we build up our skills. By adulthood we have achieved many successes and suffered numerous failures. Most of the failures matter not at all; few children at school are skilled in every mental and physical activity. We follow our own preferences, and if we intend to emphasise in one direction we must leave other avenues unexplored. And children can most certainly be harmed by over-ambitious adults who push them beyond their capabilities and breed in them this sense of failure.

But what about the things we feel we *should* do with our lives and have so far been unable to accomplish? Sometimes failure means that we must try again in order to improve on a previous attempt. That is the normal process of trial and error. But there are times when another opportunity is not given. To take an examination for a second time, for example, may be prohibited when the verdict seems to be, 'You've failed'. In this case the thing to do is not to stop and conclude we have reached a dead end in which more can be done. If we come to a barrier when trying to find our way through a maze, the obvious thing to do is to go back and look for another route. It is said that 'when one door closes, another opens'. No effort is wholly wasted, and we learn all the time from our experiences, even unpleasant ones. Failures can be turned to good; into 'stepping stones to something better'. Sir Winston Churchill failed to satisfy his schoolmasters, but became one of our greatest statesmen. Positive thoughts like these will help us to regain confidence.

Because something is rejected does not necessarily mean that it is worthless. I was amused to read that when tea was first introduced into this country, many people cooked it as they did vegetables. They boiled it in water, threw the water away and tried to eat the leaves! Similarly, those who know nothing about gems could easily discard diamonds in their raw state, thinking them to be no more than worthless lumps of rock.

Obviously, we find it more congenial to be liked and approved of by our fellows, but it is impossible to please everyone. This is illustrated by the story of the man, the boy and the donkey. A father and son set out on a long journey accompanied by their donkey. For a while, the son rode while the father led the beast along the road. Presently, they passed some fellow travellers and overheard them remark that a considerate son would not allow his aged father to walk. Hastily the boy dismounted and the father rode, until a passer-by commented that only a selfish man would force his child to walk while he travelled in comfort. Full of guilt, the man slipped from the saddle, and both he and the boy continued on foot leading the donkey. It was not long before they heard others laughing at them for walking, when to ride would have made the journey so much easier. Whereupon both man and boy mounted, only to be condemned for overworking the poor animal. In despair they decided that the only solution was to carry the donkey, but this, naturally enough, provoked universal ridicule from all who witnessed it.

We may conclude, then, that everyone will meet with disapproval from someone in the course of a lifetime. Condemnation of some action we are taking, however, is no indication that it is perforce erroneous. We must learn to have the courage of our own convictions. No one an make can accurate assessment of another's worth; it is hard enough to understand ourselves and our complex emotions. Indeed, the judgements we make of our own characters are often completely mistaken.

I was thinking recently of the Hall of Mirrors, a regular feature of the fun fairs of my youth. There were convex and concave mirrors on the walls, and as you passed by them your reflection was distorted into the most unlikely shapes, sometimes appearing long and lanky, sometimes grossly fat, or by a mixture of malformed glass, would seem to have an enormously swollen head but tiny feet, or a squat, round body with thin spindly legs like a spider. Everyone knew that these were just illusions, so it was simply a source of fun. However, this distortion of the image can occur when we try to analyse ourselves and it is then no laughing matter, for if we have a false impression of ourselves we undermine our self-confidence, feeling our natures to be inferior, inadequate and imperfect.

It is all too easy to see the negative side and overlook the positive. We forget that in nature there is a healing power at work which is able to overcome blemishes and correct errors. Dr. Leslie Weatherhead wrote:

> The trend of Nature is towards completion and perfection. My cut finger tends to heal. The scarred earth tends to become clothed in living green. The tops of my garden trees were lopped off. Soon the highest boughs, which previously were horizontal, pointed towards the sky. There was a trend towards beauty.

Similarly, we have a doctor within ourselves; a natural power in our bodies, minds and spirits, which is using our talents and traits of character and turning them towards their intended perfection and wholeness. Few of us, of course, being human and fallible, can attain such perfection, but the potential is there. In crises we often surprise ourselves and others by the way in which we act. How often we hear it said, 'I didn't think he had it in him'.

So, what of this fear we have of others' opinions? It is so easy to be mistaken in this, imagining their disapproval and censure simply because we have a low opinion of ourselves. Most of the time people are too engrossed in their own affairs to criticise the behaviour of their neighbours. A group of men during a discussion on the painting, the Mona Lisa, wondered what deep or devious thoughts could have caused that enigmatic smile. 'Probably,' said one man, 'she was just deliberating what she should have for dinner'. We cannot read the minds of others, nor they ours.

There is a gypsy proverb which states, 'Never laugh at someone because they are ignorant, for everyone knows something that you do not know'. We do not have to be clever, rich, beautiful or young to be of use in the world;

just to be ourselves and to use those qualities with we find within us. An earthenware jug can be more serviceable than a silver vase; their functions differ, but both have their place in the house. We alone are responsible for the person that we are. We must respect ourselves and seek to fulfil our potentiality. The only thing that really matters is our own integrity; the opinion of others are immaterial. A children's prayer ends with the words,

> Thank You for my eyes to see,
> Thank You, God, because I'm me.

We should, indeed, be thankful to be ourselves, and believe in ourselves.

A phrase used by the actor Denholm Elliott is worth keeping in mind,

> Surprise yourself every day with your own courage.

This is positive and hopeful thinking, which will give us back resolution and self-confidence to follow the path which we feel is right for us to take, whether or not it meets with the approval of our fellows.

8. I Don't Want to Grow Old

What is old? We may feel old at eight; young at eighty. A small child hears his eight-year old friend speaking of the wonders of the junior school and is apprehensive. What will it be like to be so 'old'? A sprightly lady of eighty decides to take an Open University course. Why not? Her mind, if not her body, is as active as ever. She is still enjoying her life and does not feel old. Age is relative. Only our bodies grow old and deteriorate with the passage of time; our minds mature, develop and increase in wisdom and understanding throughout our lives, but do not have this inbuilt retrogradation. It is said that as in every fat person there is a thin one trying to get out, so in every old man there is a young man saying, 'What on earth am I doing in here?'

We are such curiously dissatisfied creatures. When we are young we yearn to be older; yet, on reaching maturity, we long to return again to the days of our youth. Few children would agree with their elders' oft repeated remark that our schooldays are the happiest of our lives. I remember my elderly employer, when I first started work, telling me how fortunate I was to have all my life before me. To me it seemed a futile remark; after all, he had not been deprived of his own youth. Indeed, I felt that I had more cause for complaint than he, because my adolescence coincided with the war years, not by any means a time for carefree gaiety.

Shakespeare spoke of the seven ages of man, each stage of development being sharply defined and each having its own distinct characteristicss. In a few lines he makes this skilful exemplification, giving us a vivid picture of man's changing nature from infancy to old age. He does not portray man as being happy in any stage of his life; the baby cries, the boy hates school, the young man is disappointed in love and obliged to serve as a soldier, in middle age he is complacent and bored, the retired man petulant and disgruntled, while in old age he paints a gloomy picture of a geriatric state of disability and degeneration, such as, I suppose, most people dread when they say that they fear growing old.

This, I think, is to take altogether too pessimistic a view. Undoubtedly there will be many who become senile in extreme old age, but the majority of us will retain our faculties and our capacity for enjoyment throughout our lives.

But, of course, there is much truth in what Shakespeare wrote and there can be good reasons for our discontent. The school child envies the infant who remains at home to be cossetted, but he many fear the restrictions of the more demanding years ahead of him. The youth resents being told what to do by parents and employers and chafes at the law's limitation of his freedom. While rejoicing in his boundless energy, he is none the less haunted by fears of growing less virile, being too old for his chosen sport or to participate in the pursuits of his colleagues. It seems that for only a very few years will he enjoy his youthful prime; what then remains of life presents a barren and worthless prospect. The middle-aged man longs for his lost youth and vitality and dreads the illness and deterioration of his declining years. And, when old age itself approaches and most of his relatives and acquaintances have died, he feels helpless, lonely and, like Shakespeare's man at his seventh age, as if he is entering a period of absolute loss and oblivion. But what a gloomy and negative subsistence it would be if life consisted only of loss, misery, inhibition and despair; and existence entirely devoid of hope. Thankfully, we have within us a spirit of freedom that can rise

above our bodily limitations, bringing us joy and contentment and taking no account of age. The happiest people
are those who are able to live in the present and to be
satisfied with their lot; who can say with St Paul, 'I have
learned, in whatsoever state I am, therewith to be content'.

At whatever stage in our lives we may be, from youth to
maturity, it is tempting to look back with regret to days
when we were younger, or forward with apprehension of
what the future may bring. Such nostalgia for the past or
speculation about the future is pointless, for we can only
live in the present.

Memories of the present are notoriously unreliable. We
tend to recall only the pleasanter times; days when the sun
shone and we were happy and free from care. Were we
able to return to them we should almost certainly find
flaws in those old delights, for in the intervening years we
ourselves have developed and matured, the world about us
has changed and our judgements and critical faculties have
sharpened and become more sensitive. If, for example, we
see again an old film which thrilled us in our teens, we are
now likely to find it tawdry, badly presented, the
characters lacking in depth and the plot unconvincing.
When we long for the past, with its less crowded roads, its
friendly corner shops, its cheerful coal fires and more
leisurely pace of life, we tend to forget the terrible poverty
of the under-privileged, the bitter winters without adequate heating, the suffering through lack of modern drugs,
the long hours of work, the drudgery of household labour,
and the plight of so many women, worn out by constant
child-bearing and entirely dependent on their husbands for
food and shelter. There is much, after all, to be said for the
present day. I am certainly grateful for the comfort of cen-
tral heating, the convenience of gas and electricity in the
home, the possibilities of travel, and for being able, as a
single woman, to have had a career and independence.
Shelley wrote,

> We look before and after,
> And pine for what is not

We are so preoccupied with the past and the future that we often fail to appreciate and enjoy the present. Daily and monthly horoscopes appear in most newspapers and periodicals and are eagerly scanned. I must admit that I quite enjoy reading mine, but it is a mistake to take them too seriously, particularly if they prophesy disaster. I have known those whose lives were ruined because some fortune-teller spoke of misfortune of ill health to come. African witch doctors exert such influence over those who believe in them, that the victim of a death cure will sicken and die, not through any bodily disease, but because he is literally frightened to death. The subconscious mind is very powerful. If we expect and fear a miserable old age we are well on the way to building such a future for ourselves. The optimistic person looks for and usually finds the best in life. Naturally, illnesses and disabilities will come to all of us, but the way in which we cope with them will make all the difference and we should seek to 'meet all ills and cross-accidents with gallant and high-hearted happiness'.

Life is a progression and a purposeful journey. Why should we seek to turn back? We do not know what lies ahead, and it is foolish to suppose that only evils and disappointments lie around the next bend in the road. Let us keep our spirit of adventure and go on boldly, ready to meet the challenges before us. Some elderly folk say, 'What is left to me? My life is almost over; I have nothing to look forward to'. They see death as a blank wall; not a closed door. I believe that we go on through death and that, as Browning said, 'the best is yet to be'.

All nature confirms this belief. We see old age as the winter of our lives, a hard time when our energy is low and happy and untroubled days behind us. But winter does not disintegrate into oblivion and nothingness; it is the preparation for spring and new birth, for rejuvenation, hope and vigorous growth. Even in winter, a tree remains beautiful, its bare boughs revealing its shape and true character, while, within itself, it is nurturing the blossoms

and leaves of a renewed life. So why should we despair and
assume that it is only the early stages of our lives that are
worth living?

If we fear old age, let us consider its advantages as well
as its drawbacks. The old have the accumulated wisdom
and experience of a lifetime; they have learned to understand themselves and to come to terms with life and its
hazards. They have built up self-confidence and have
discovered the mode of living best suited to themselves.
They can draw on a vast store of happy memories from
past years, and most have the comfort of children and
grandchildren and the satisfaction of seeing them grow up
and take their place in the world. Most of all, they have
time at their disposal, no longer having to be ruled by the
clock; time in which to think, to meditate, to cultivate
serenity and peace of mind. If we can achieve this, there is
little to be feared in old age and, far from being useless, the
old can fill a vital role in giving inspiration to the young.

> As a candle
> In a holy place,
> Such is the beauty
> Of an aged face,

This is how we should see growing old.

We cannot shut our eyes to the afflictions of age; they
may indeed beset us. But troubles can overwhelm us at any
stage of our life. Let us then go forward with hope and
courage, let us enjoy today, and await tomorrow with
confidence and trust, for we can all remain eternally young
in heart.

9. There's no Pleasure in Life. I can't ever be Happy

Happiness is not ours by right. We should not feel aggrieved if we are denied it. Many make it their sole objective in life, but seldom find it. If we seek only self-gratification and pleasure we are nearly always disillusioned; it is like chasing a rainbow; we glimpse it afar off, but it fades away before we can touch it.

Love was once described in a song as 'a bright, elusive butterfly'. Happiness is even more elusive and even more diligently sought for. It does not come easily. Plenty of money, perfect health, everything we need; none of these guarantees it; indeed I know two people one of whom has multiple sclerosis and the other who is blind, yet both are extremely happy. Although they have less that most of us, they seem to have discovered the secret of happiness. How can it be achieved? When we feel that we have found it, it all too often seems to slide from our grasp.

The novelist Vicky Baum once wrote,

"If it lasted, it wouldn't be happiness any more. If it were our daily bread, we wouldn't appreciate it. Happiness cannot be forced, or coaxed, or commanded. It comes all by itself and everyone can be sure to get a share. But this share may be a little bigger if we are ready to be happy; ready and relaxed and willing to recognise the rare bird when it alights in our heart."

There is a great deal of truth in this. Real happiness

usually lasts only briefly, but because of its rarity is all the more to be treasured. Most people would settle for contentment or peace of mind as a satisfactory substitute. Certainly they can come near to happiness.

Contentment can be gained by absorbing ourselves in work that needs to be done, Recently, among graffiti on a blank wall, someone had scrawled in large letters, I HATE WORK. This, I felt, was a sad comment. The road to happiness is to find satisfaction in work; to carry it out to the best of our ability, so that we are putting back into the world our now positive contribution, our thank offering for the gift of life, the privileges of sight, hearing and touch, the pleasures of food and drink, love and companionship. We are made to do and to create; to use our skills to subscribe to the well-being of the whole human family. In centuries past, when life was simpler and people lived in small village communities, this was self-evident. The hunters and farmers provided food, millers prepared the corn, blacksmiths and potters made tools and utensils, weavers and spinners the clothes, and so on. Each had his allotted task; all gave and all received, and, when the work was done, enjoyed their leisure times together. Nowadays, when so much work is routine and repetitive and when for many there is no work at all, it is easy to lose sight of this idea of contributing to the community. Yet it still remains true. No one owes us a living; to enjoy life we must give back to life. If the work we do is dull, it none the less needs to be carried out. If we can find no paid employment, we must, for our own sake as well as that of others, search out worthwhile ways of occupying ourselves in some service to our fellows. Then only will we be able to enjoy our hours of relaxation feeling that they have been earned and merited.

If we are going through a period of illness, sorrow or anxiety, we may feel, indeed, that life can offer us nothing in the way of pleasure. But every dark time passes. Life is a strange and complex mixture of joys and sorrows, pleasures and pains. Browning wrote a great deal about the meaning of life. One of his conclusions was,

> For life, with all its yields of joy and woe
> And hope and fear, – believe the aged friend –
> Is just a chance o' the prize of learning love.

Perhaps he is right. We can only learn to love by living; by experiencing it, not by reading about it or reasoning with our minds; love not just of man for woman, but love of children, love of our families, love of mankind itself, the world we live in, and love of God. Such love may bring pain, but it is only by loving that we find pleasure in life and, indeed, our true happiness. Thomas Traherne expressed this more profoundly,

> You never enjoy the world aright, till the sea itself floweth in your veins, till you are clothed with the heavens and crowned with the stars; and perceive yourself to be the sole heir of the whole world and more than so, because men are in it who are every one sole heirs as well as you. Till you can sing and rejoice and delight in God, as misers do in gold, and kings in sceptres, you never enjoy the world.

We can learn so much from nature. If we consider the birds, we can see that despite the hazards and dangers they are exposed to, birds appear to enjoy living. If we watch the way in which they fly, we will notice that many birds make use of the wind to hold them up, gliding down the breeze as we would free-wheel down hill on a bicycle. Gulls frequently do this. Another fascinating thing is the formation in which flocks of birds frequently fly. One leads and the others fan out behind it in two lines, spreading gradually outwards in the shape of a V. This also is because they are using the wind currents set up by the leading bird. They are making the effort of flying easier for themselves, and this could be a wise precaution if they are travelling for long distances. The strongest bird takes the lead; the less able use the easier track. When life is hard, we should follow their example and be kind to ourselves. This does not mean giving in and doing nothing. We should try to carry on, but be content to take life at a slower pace, letting others help us if we feel unable to take the initiative. Too often we force ourselves to go beyond our physical strength. It is wiser to slow down for a while.

Birds give us the example of early rising. There is great satisfaction in being up with the dawn on a spring or summer morning. The world seems fresh and new, and to be up betimes gets us off to a good start and sets the tone to the day. Birdsong is one of the delights of spring. To cultivate the habit of cheerfulness is no bad thing and can carry us though many a trying time. Of course, birdsong, beautiful through it is, is not just an expression of the joy of living. For them it is the way they establish their territory, very necessary when they are defending the area which will provide their food. Singing, for birds, is the carrying on of their normal daily life, and if we set ourselves to do this, as far as we are able, it will certainly help to lessen our feelings of unhappiness. However bad the weather, the birds continue to sing. The storm-cock, in fact, sings its loudest when rain is falling; a sort of defiance against adversity perhaps. Attitude of mind is all-important.

To remain healthy a bird must keep its feathers in good condition. They are vital for its flight and warmth, and birds are continually preening, smoothing and washing them. When we feel low it is very tempting to neglect our appearance. A man will go unshaven; a woman will not bother with make-up. How easy it is to lounge around the house in a dressing gown to save the effort of dressing, to neglect hair and clothes and simply feel, 'What does it matter?' But this will only make us more dissatisfied with life.

A final thought on the subject of birds. The most wonderful of all their activities is their migration. Why is it necessary? Some birds, living in a land of plenty, will leave it each year and fly thousands of miles to a colder climate in which to nest. We do not know all the reasons, but it is obviously needful for their continued survival. We too need to vary our lives, to take a break, a holiday, or a change of occupation from time to time to prevent us from growing stale. And how do birds find their way over such vast areas of sea and land? Again, we can only guess, but somehow they are guided by instinct and will even return to the same nest year after year. We also need a sense of direction in our lives, so that we feel purpose and hope in living. This, for most of us, is our religious faith and our belief in God's guidance. Even without such faith, we can believe in life itself. One tiny swallow will travel from Africa on a journey that we should find arduous in a plane. It will build its nest here; we will hear its song and be glad that summer has come. If its life is so precious, then every human life must be even more so. It is only our low spirits that cause us to feel that there is no pleasure in life.

It may be that we find our lives drab and unsatisfying because we are constantly seeking thrills and excitement and expecting to be involved in momentous events. We should find greater satisfaction if we could turn our minds from larger matters and try to concentrate for a while on the very small and trivial. It is said that 'small is beautiful', and so, indeed, it can be. Children have this knack of occupying their minds for hours at a time with something that has fascinated them. A child will blow soap bubbles perhaps, or watch ants running to and fro in the garden, completely oblivious of the passage of time or anything that is happening around him.

Here are some suggestions on how to discover pleasure for a while in the little things of life:

Make a cup of tea. Sit down and drink it slowly. Really enjoy and savour it. Appreciate the warmth of the cup between your fingers and the soothing effect of the tea as you sip it. Think of the tea bush growing in the hot sunshine, and all the processes the leaves pass through before reaching the packet in the shop where you bought it. Consider how lucky we are to have tea, with its reviving and refreshing qualities. Remember how, when it was first imported here, it was so precious that it was kept in a special locked caddy tables. Now it is our everyday drink. The Japanese make tea drinking a leisurely and ceremonious occasion, and we too should allow ourselves longer to enjoy our teatime, instead of just snatching a quick cup between jobs. We need to give the tea a chance to relax us, as it will if we will let it.

Find a single flower, any will do, either a wild or a garden one. A daisy, for example, would be easy enough to find on the garden lawn. Now really examine it and enjoy its beauty. See how delicate its colouring is, and how fragile its petals. How wonderfully it is shaped and how well equipped to withstand whatever extremes of weather may come. Try to draw or even paint it. It doesn't matter if you are no artist; the fact of attempting to copy its beauty will impress it upon your mind and emphasise your feelings of appreciation.

If it is raining so that you cannot go out and the gloomy day has even further oppressed you, go to the window and look at the raindrops for a while. Find one at the top and trace its passage down the pane with your finger. Then do the same with the others. Note how they mingle together, gaining momentum as they race down the glass. It is fascinating to watch the tracks they take and to see how beautiful they are as the light catches them. It may be a childish pastime, but it is a positive one, far better than sitting doing nothing and allowing despondent thoughts to take over.

Find something in the house to mend, polish or improve in some way. Choose something you like, so that to improve its appearance is a pleasure, not a duty. This again is a positive action, creating beauty or restoring use.

Take time to look at clouds. Follow their slow passage

through the sky, observe their shapes subtly changing, and the way some move faster than others. Notice their colours and that of the sky behind them. Let your thoughts drift with the clouds. This is a form of meditation and very beneficial.

Find something that needs sorting; a box of buttons, jewellery, cottons, a tool box, string or wool bag, and restore it to order. This will help to relax your mind.

Concentrate on tiny sounds or movements within the room. The tick of the clock is a companionable thing, and if you are lucky enough to have a wood or coal fire, the gentle rush of flickering flames and the soft plop of the ash is very soothing. Watch the sparks, the smoke spiralling upwards, or any other slowly moving object such as fish in a tank.

All these are trivial things, of course; you will be able to think of many others. They may seem unimportant, but by concentrating on them, rather than on thoughts of gloom and despair, you will find in small measure some satisfaction again in life.

Contentment and peace of mind are two vital ingredients of happiness. It is worth our while to cultivate such an attitude.

> Life owes me nothing; one clear morn
> Is boon enough for being born.
> And be it ninety years or ten
> No need for me to question when.
> My life is mine, I find it good,
> And greet each hour with gratitude.
>
> *Anon.*

It is really a question, I think of looking at the world with selective eyes, seeing not only its sorrows and miseries, the violence, hatred and greed, the wars and famines, but also the beauty, goodness and love which are everywhere present. When we are in a despairing mood we see only the bad; yet good far outweighs evil. Elizabeth

Barrett Browning wrote:

> There are nettles everywhere
> But smooth, green grasses are more common still
> The blue of heaven is larger than the cloud.

So, if we feel disheartened and are finding the going hard, let us resolve to have a more positive outlook; to plod on with our daily tasks, not looking for happiness, but finding satisfaction in doing the best we are able. Let us use our leisure time to relax and enjoy the small and commonplace comforts. Let us put into life all we can, not for reward, but in gratitude for life itself, that most precious of all gifts. Let us try to be content with what we have, holding on to hope, for it is through hope that happiness itself can, at last, be found.

> True hope is swift, and flies with swallows' wings;
> Kings it makes gods, and meaner creatures kings.
> *Shakespeare* (King Richard III)

10. Other People haven't had my Troubles

There are times in life when we find ourselves beset by constant misfortune. No sooner do we recover from one mishap, that another disaster strikes. Troubles, they say, never come singly, and we can well believe it. At times like these we feel that nothing will ever go right again, and it is hard indeed not to envy our friends and neighbours who seem to lead tranquil lives without the burden of worry and care which weighs us down so greivously. It is easy to feel resentful. 'Why should this happen to me? What have I done to deserve such misery? Why can't I have an easy life like my friends?'

Most of us can cope with short periods of adversity. It is when the problem seems to have no solution, when we are expected to bear burdens beyond our strength, that we begin to lose hope and feel that we can no longer carry on. It this situation we must look for help; to struggle on will only result in a breakdown of our own health. There is always someone to whom we can turn, whether a friend who can offer sympathy and advice, or someone who, in an official capacity, can provide a measure of relief for the situation in which we find ourselves.

Caring for sick or elderly relatives, problems of drugs, drink or antisocial behaviour within the family, or our own failing health can all impose heavy burdens. Sometimes there may be no cure. It may be facing the fact that an illness, our own or that of someone we love, is terminal, or a marriage may have broken down irretrievably. If this is the case we have to accept and come to terms with the inevitable. There is no other option. Resentment, bitterness and frustration will only add to our hurt.

Equally harmful is the way in which we so often nurse grudges against others who have injured us in some way, hugging to ourselves the memories of past wrongs and allowing them to fester and rankle in our minds. There is a story of a hunter who left a kettle unattended on his cooking fire. A bear wandered into the camp and, being curious at the sight of steam issuing from the kettle's spout, put out a paw to touch it. This resulted in a painful scald, which angered the bear so that he hit out at the kettle. Naturally enough, he only burned himself again so, perceiving the kettle as an enemy that was attacking him, his instinctive reaction was to seize the offending adversary and hug it to himself as hard as he could. Obviously, this injured him far worse than before, just as we will harm only ourselves if we persist in hugging our resentments.

There is no panacea for curing all troubles; they will not dissolve and vanish overnight; rather we have to learn how to cope with them, to ride out the storm until they are over. There are many ways in which we can do this and make life easier. Nature often points the way.

I was walking, in late summer, along a rather dingy back street, when I happened to look up at the roof of a derelict house and was astonished to see a large plant growing out of the broken down gutter. Some accumulated rubble and brick dust would have settled there, and it had established itself in this unlikely soil. Despite such discouraging conditions, it appeared to be thriving. Not only were its leaves and branches strong and healthy, but it had produced long spikes of beautiful purple flowers, which hung down partly camouflaging the ugly ruin of the building. It was a buddleia. Later that day I saw another buddleia on a tumble-down wall, and yet another thrusting through a narrow crack between a pavement and a shed, and I found myself thinking what a remarkable plant it is.

Any gardener knows how easily the most cherished

flowers will die if they are deprived of the conditions they enjoy or are exposed to the slightest hardship; just a touch of frost, an east wind, too little or too much sun, an invasion of greenfly, a visit from a family of slugs, and they are gone. Yet, despite all opposition, the buddleia appears to flourish. Indeed, it may be that it actually owes its strength to those poor circumstances in which it so often finds itself. It has been obliged to develop strong stems and tough leaves to cope with them. And yet, the surprising thing is that it is not an ugly, gaunt and rugged plant which no one would care to cultivate, but can produce such beautiful flowers that it is the main source of attraction to many of our lovliest butterflies. The buddleia is often known as 'the butterfly bush', and for that reason is a popular garden shrub. Another of its features is that the harder it is pruned in the autumn, the more strongly it will grow and the more flowers it will bear in the following year.

It may be that we can learn something from the buddleia. It is natural when tribulation comes to think, 'I can't go on like this. I might as well give up'. These are negative thoughts and will produce the same result as a hot-house plant shrivelling in the frost. The buddleia, when exposed to adverse conditions, reacts in three ways, and I think we should try to do the same. It grows a strong root and stems. Our roots are our belief in ourselves and in God, our determination not to give in, and our conviction that eventually we will overcome our problems. Our branches are our willingness to carry on with life, accepting its present limitations, but aiming to take a positive attitude, moving forward slowly, step by step, until our difficulties are behind us.

The buddleia grows thick, tough leaves. We have to learn to be strong, to shoulder our responsibilities, to refuse to give in to fears and pressures, and to resolve never to give up hope.

The buddleia brings into being beautiful flowers which butterflies prefer to any others in the garden. This, of course, is quite unexpected. How can any good come out of trouble? And yet it CAN. It does depend on us. We can react to it with resentment, or give up in despair. We can be like the hot-house plants of we wish to be. But we don't have to. We all have the potential of the buddleia stock and we can react to trouble in a positive way.

It can develop in us a deeper understanding of and compassion for others, and a greater awareness of how to cope with our own weaknesses. It can teach us patience and tolerance and, when the bad times are over, a keener appreciation of the joy of living and the wonder of the universe. Just as the flowers of the buddleia attract butterflies to feed from its nectar, so we can be of help to others because of our experience of life's suffering.

No one would choose to have troubles. Every plant, if given a choice, would opt for a carefully tilled and fertile garden in which to grow. But it is often found that plants cultivated in too rich a soil will produce mainly leaves and only very poor flowers. It is those that have to struggle for survival which bear the most beautiful blooms. I do not think that trouble is a punishment inflicted upon us by God, nor that any illness or misfortune is deliberately 'sent to try us'. What is important is our attitude to our afflictions and our determination to overcome them. A positive attitude will enable us to say,

> Let me use disappointment as material for
> patience,
> Let me use suspense as material for
> perseverence,
> Let me use danger as material for courage,
> Let me use pain as material for endurance.

This may seem impossible when we are at our lowest ebb. Nevertheless, we should try to look at our problems in this light, remembering the improbability of the buddleia surviving in the ruined gutter and its amazing triumph over its limitations.

It is the right approach to our troubles that will help us

to cope with them. I have discovered that the old, familiar children's game of Ludo can teach us a great deal about contending with all the vicissitudes of life. When children play it they learn to count, to recognise the numbers on the dice, to play fairly, not to expect to win every time, and to enjoy the thrill of competition and uncertainty. As adults, we can learn even more valuable lessons, I think, and particularly when misfortune has made us uncertain of ourselves and life has become confusing and even frightening.

To commence the game of Ludo each player waits until a six is thrown. This may come speedily or be long delayed, but no move can be made without it. Following a six, a second throw is allowed. How true this is of life. 'Nothing succeeds like success', we say, for having done well we are encouraged to make even further progress. Successful people can forge ahead and the way is smoothed for them. But in adversity it is as if the dice will give us every number but the six. We see the world hurrying past and we are so loaded down by care that we are unable to keep up. This is where, like the Ludo player, we have to learn patience. The six remains in its place on the dice, and in due course it must appear.

During a game of Ludo it often happens that one or two players with continual high scores will press ahead, making rapid progress round the board while their opponents can only struggle slowly. It is true of life that there seem to be unequal opportunities; some must work harder than others, some appear to have more than their share of troubles while their neighbours escape. But in the game there are few who avoid being 'sent back home' at some point or other, and the dice will bring sudden and unexpected swings of fortune. Life is a great compensator and the human body has a wonderful capacity for adapting to change. Once misfortunes are past it is even possible to see that some good has come out of them. It is only when we are in the depths of despair that we feel we shall continue in this state for the rest of our lives.

There is a certain amount of skill in playing even a simple game like Ludo. Children soon learn that it is not all a matter of chance, and that it is wiser to have two or three counters in play rather than to concentrate on getting a single one round the board quickly. If disaster comes and that counter is returned to base, they may have to wait for a long time and waste valuable turns before a six on the dice enables them to start again. Similarly we need to work out the best way of easing our own troubles, avoiding if possible any situation which will make them worse and bring about a setback from which we may take a long time to recover.

Disasters occur in Ludo; counters are returned to the beginning again, and how frustrating this can be if they have almost reached the safety of 'home'., However, such mishaps are soon put right. The counter is sent on its way again however many times it is to re-start. So we must keep on trying and never give up hope when we are struggling to escape from our problems. A setback is disappointing, but never hopeless. We just have to begin again, no matter how discouraged we may feel.

It is worth noticing that each counter in the game is a different colour and each aims for its own goal. We can sometimes make life more difficult for ourselves by trying to copy other people's ways of living. We all vary in character and ability and have to pursue the path that is right for us. We must, of course, have a goal to aim for, otherwise it is pointless to make progress along a path that leads us nowhere. When we have troubles we should try to plan ahead for the time when they are over. We may be unable to take any action at all in the prevailing circumstances, but the very fact of thinking positively will bring nearer the time when we can do so.

A Ludo board has carefully marked out tracks along which each counter must travel before it reaches its home base. I firmly believe that there is a purpose in our lives; that we are free to go forwards or backwards or to stand still, but although we often fail to see it, especially when we are weighed down by troubles, we have a right path to follow in the world and a final destination for which life is the preparation.

It is comforting to notice that the coloured squares which mark the end of the counters' journey are safe areas. Once there they cannot be harmed until they reach their home. Troubles can bring about much fear. We feel threatened on every side and we instinctively want to hide and make no further effort. Certainly life is no bed of roses, and we do have to face difficulties and even dangers as we journey onwards. But there are still happy and carefree days, laughter and pleasure, the love and companionship of friends and children, husbands and wives. Problems may come, causing us to be cut off from these, but they will pass. If we have faith in God's love and protection we will still feel shielded and guided even when trouble is at its worst. If the players in the Ludo game continue for long enough every counter on the board will safely reach its home. This is the secret; to persevere, however long it takes, believing that, in the end, all will be well. St Teresa once wrote:

> Let nothing disturb thee
> Let nothing dismay thee
> All things pass.

It is no consolation, when we have troubles, to compare our lot with that of others and complain that our burden is greater. No one can go through life unscathed; we all experience some illness, sorrow, pain, loneliness and fear. We can best overcome our misfortunes by learning to rise above them, refusing to let them discourage and defeat us, and by believing that they will eventually be surmounted. This is where hope will show us the way.

> No rock so hard but that a little wave
> May beat submission in a thousand years.

11. I'm Depressed and I can't cope with Life

"Depression", wrote a doctor, "is without doubt the most unpleasant experience known to man." Anyone who has been through a depressive illness would wholeheartedly agree with him. It is, of all states, the one in which hope seems furthest away; we are plunged into the depths of despair and misery. But there are three very hopeful and positive things to hold on to when we are at our lowest ebb:

1. Depression always goes. It may be prolonged, but it does not last for ever.
2. It can do us no harm physically. It may produce pain, but it is an illness of the mind and cannot damage any part of our bodies.
3. When the depression is over we will find it has strengthened us, deepened our understanding of others and made us more appreciative of the joy of living.

There are also three things which depression does not do. It does not make us mad; many people fear this unnecessarily. It does not denote weakness of character; Sir Winston Churchill and Florence Nightingale both suffered from it and can hardly be regarded as weaklings. It does not disappear overnight; we cannot just 'snap out of it'. Clinical depression, as opposed to just feeling miserable, always requires a fairly long period of recuperation.

When we become depressed we are in a very confused state of mind, but our feelings can be summed up as fear and exhaustion, not knowing how to cope with life, and the sensation of being trapped in a long, dark tunnel. We will consider these in turn, and the ways in which we can ease the depression and hasten its cure.

The first thing to do is to bring ourselves to accept it and to overcome our fears. Imagine a bather who finds himself in difficulties. He has come further than he intended from the shore and, although he is a reasonable enough swimmer, he is becoming exhausted. The best thing he can do is to turn on his back and float for a while. If the tide is coming in it will bring him nearer to the shore without his having to make further effort. Even if it is not, it will allow him to rest and regain energy for another attempt, or, at the very least, will enable him to stay afloat until help arrives. Were he to continue to struggle on swimming, he would inevitably use up all his resources and drown.

In depression we are in a similar situation. Carrying on with life has become as exhausting to us as swimming to the man trying to regain the shore. So often we endeavour to redouble our efforts to maintain our usual standards to keep pace with our colleagues and to hide our feelings of inadequacy and weariness. This only results in a worsening of the depression and we find we are fighting a losing battle. Depression makes life more difficult. It is as if we have to walk through deep water, while everyone else trips easily along on dry land. Wading through deep water IS possible; progress can be made and even be pleasurable, but attempting to run through it is foolish and can be disastrous. In depression we just have to slow down.

To return to the idea of the swimmer. In order to float he has to do several things. First he takes the decision to stop swimming and float instead. Then he must turn over onto his back, stop the movements of his arms and legs, allow the water to support him and trust it to do so. In depression we must first decide to change our attitude to life for a while, accept the fact that we are depressed, stop struggling to maintain impossibly high standards and be content with only the essentials. We have to give ourselves time to rest and relax. Spring cleaning, major decisions, and non-urgent business matters can be postponed, some tasks delegated and some problems solved by consultation with others. We must lighten the work load and the pressure for the time being. If we do not, we just build up tension and frustration in ourselves because we find we are unable to cope.

A friend once gave me a lift in his car and, being in a hurry, I got in quickly and gave the seat belt a jerk to pull it down and fasten it. I couldn't understand why it would not move until my friend explained, "You have to pull it gently. If you jerk it, it automatically locks, because this is how it would react to a jerk in an accident". And this is how we have to react to depression. Go gently. If we try to force ourselves on, we come to standstill. Going gently means that we must proceed at a slower pace, but we do keep going, and by slowing down we are allowing ourselves to build up our reserves of strength. In time we will be able to return to a quicker speed. So we must learn to accept our limitations calmly, stop worrying, and try to relax until the depression passes.

To force ourselves to pause when we are involved in the rate race of modern living is by no means easy, but in the long run we find that we can more than catch up if we allow ourselves periods in which to renew our energy. If we are depressed this slowing down becomes essential. When driving a car at a steady rate, we may notice other drivers who race past as if they cannot bear to have anyone ahead of them. Yet, when we reach traffic lights or railway crossing gates, we are just behind them and they have really gained nothing for all their feverish efforts.

When the poet Milton lost his sight he worried because he could no longer carry out the duties which he felt that God required of him. It was only when he had come to terms with his blindness that he was able to realise and to write: "They also serve who only stand and wait." So we must accept our depression and allow ourselves to float through it without frustration and resentment, and patiently wait for it to pass. Once we have recovered we will find that we can tackle life's tasks again with renewed energy and enthusiasm.

Learning how to cope with the depression itself is the next priority. Naturally, we are eager to be rid of it as soon as possible, yet few illnesses have an instant cure. Even for something as trivial as a cut finger, we have to give the body a chance to heal itself; it will not be hurried.

All the same, we ourselves can do a great deal to help that healing process. Consider what happens if we do cut a finger. It might be so slight an injury that it needs nothing more than a quick wash under the cold tap, or it may be deep enough to entail a visit to hospital for stitches. The three stages of treatment would normally be: to clean, disinfect and, if necessary, treat the wound; to apply a bandage or plaster to keep it clean; and to protect it from further injury. All three steps can be taken in our treatment of depression which, like a cut finger or any other injury, will vary from being slight to severe and must be dealt with accordingly.

Just as it would be foolish to ignore a badly cut finger and run the risk of its turning septic, so we must not disregard the symptoms of depression. They are signs that all is not well with us; perhaps we are illtreating our body by subjecting it to too much stress, or we may need to change our life style to one more suited to our temperament. We need to discover what is causing the depression, and if possible remove that cause. If a nail protruding from a piece of furniture was responsible for the cut finger, the commonsense thing would be to hammer it in and render it harmless. If we cut ourselves on the sharp edge of a time we will be more careful in the future when using the tin opener. But, once the damage has been done, we have to set about assisting the healing process. So we will consider how we can best recover from depression by thinking about it in terms of a cut finger.

CLEAN, DISINFECT AND TREAT. Depression can be treated in a number of ways. Most important, perhaps, is to learn how to relax the tension which it invariably builds up in us. Taking tranquillisers will do this for a time, but because they are addictive should not be continued over a long period, unless the doctor advises it for some specific reason. It is far better to learn relaxation for ourselves by taking life more slowly, trying breathing exercises, relaxation cassettes and so on. A holiday will often help to soothe and calm us and break the build up of pressure. Even a few days away from the usual routine can work wonders. It is important to eat well-balanced meals. We need all the body's resources to fight depression, and although we may feel tired and have little appetite, it is essential to prepare good, nourishing food. It need not be an elaborate meal, but a diet of tea and buns will soon weaken our natural resistance. Just as deep cuts need more expert treatment than the home First Aid box, so serious depression may need the help of a doctor or psychiatrist, or even a stay in hospital. Do not be afraid of this. The psychiatrist is the specialist in the field of depression, and the doctor will refer you to him if he is unable to cure your depression himself.

APPLY A BANDAGE. A bandage or plaster will stop a cut from bleeding and help to keep it clean, so hastening the healing process. We can shorten the duration of our depression in a number of ways. Very often, if we examine our lives, we find that we are either driving ourselves too hard, or that we are bored by having insufficient to do. Either extreme can bring on depression. It is sometimes a good thing to set ourselves a quota of jobs to do each day, taking care that we do not fix an impossibly high target. We should always allow ourselves periods of relaxation when we can indulge in a hobby or just put our feet up. Hobbies are very helpful; they distract our minds from concentrating on the depression and going round and round like a mouse in a treadmill. It helps to understand more about depression, so that we can think of it as merely another illness, which it is, and not blame ourselves for being as we are. Many who have a sincere religious faith have found this an excellent bandage. It is not a magic cure; indeed many deeply religious people go through times of depression, but it does make the pain more bearable and certainly prevents it from festering and making us bitter and resentful. Avoiding certain foods and habits which aggravate depression, such as over-dependence on alcohol, cigarettes or too much coffee or tea will also help us. Finally, if we are lucky enough to have understanding friends who will not brush aside our symptoms as trivial figments of our imagination, or self-indulgence, we will find their support invaluable. Sadly, depression is so very often misunderstood, even by families and lifelong friends.

PROTECTION FROM FURTHER INJURY. When the depression starts to lift, this is the time to take precautions to ensure that it will not recur. We should try again to check that we are not driving ourselves too hard, and until the depression is really a thing of the past, avoid, for example reading sad books, watching traumatic television programmes, and, wherever possible, endeavour to keep away from stressful situations, and concentrate on the good and positive side of life. Thinking positively needs considerable practice, but it is worth working at until it becomes a habit. As soon as we wake in the morning we should think of all the good things that will be materialising in the day ahead. We should never nurse a grudge or feeling of anger. These emotions can be terribly destructive and feed depression. It is far better to have it out with the person who is causing the resentment. If this is impossible, we should try to dismiss it from our minds, or work out our frustration by a bit of hard work in the house or garden or a long energetic walk, swim or game.

Thirdly, if we have accepted that we are depressed, and must learn to cope with it to the best of our ability, it is still very hard to struggle on through that dark and lonely tunnel. How can we keep going?

Some months ago, I went for a short trip by barge along one of the canals. It was a pleasant change from bus or train; so much more relaxed and peaceful. I was very interested when we went through a long tunnel. The towing path stopped abruptly here, and we were told that when all barges were horse-drawn, the horses made a detour and rejoined the barge at the far end. The bargees had to propel their craft themselves by 'legging' it through. This was a most laborious and, I should imagine, uncomfortable process. They had to lie on their backs and walk with their legs against the wall for the whole length of the tunnel.

The barge I travelled in was engine-powered, and the tunnel well lit by electricity. How different it must have been in the days of the leggers. If the tunnel was of any length, it would have been an eerie experience struggling in the pitch darkness to work the barge along, your feet pressing against the damp, slippery walls and, for a long time, no light ahead to prove that your efforts were having any appreciable effect. What a contrast to the pleasant drifting through sunny buttercup meadows, with a couple of patiently plodding horses taking the strain as they made their way steadily along the towing path.

This going through a tunnel well describes our experience of depression, and is as dramatic a contrast to normal living, which resembles the journey through open country. The horses which pull us along are our feelings of hope and expectancy, our ambitions, our belief in the goodness of life and of our ability to cope with its ups and downs. Then the tunnel comes, the horses disappear, and we are left alone in the darkness with nothing but our own determination to get us through.

This is the important thing to remember. We have to want to overcome the depression and to be willing to do something about it. 'Legging' is hard work and often seems to bring no results, but we have to keep at it, believing that in the end those efforts will bring about the outcome we long for. There is no easy cure for depression and we each have to discover for ourselves the things which will lessen it for us, because what helps one does not necessarily act in the same way for another. Once these are found, we must patiently work at them, knowing that, eventually, we shall come through that tunnel and into the light at the other end.

Depression can be a very frightening experience, and plunging into a dark tunnel is certainly a good description of it. I think it helps if we remember that the tunnel is there for a purpose, perhaps going through dangerous territory, or under a steep hill, and that the walls which shut us in and cause us so much fear, are actually there for our protection. Because a tunnel has been built and has a beginning, it must have an end. Leggers would feel that every painstaking step was taking them nearer to that end. They knew that, because the water was flowing onwards and because countless others had been that way before them, there was no need to fear to venture into its dark entrance. It is the same in depression; many, many others have passed this way before us; life is flowing on, it is an unpleasant experience, but we need not fear it.

Strange though it may seem, depression CAN sometimes be a protection, just as the tunnel walls are. In some cases, if we have been exposed to an unbearable degree of stress, the onset of depression prevents us from carrying on as we had done before. It forces us to change our life style. It brings us up short and makes us realise that something is wrong; perhaps we are outdoing our strength, being over-ambitious, or trying to reach an impossible goal. It certainly slows us down, and this may be no bad thing.

It is the darkness of the tunnel which is the hardest to bear. The old leggers had no electricity, but perhaps they would carry flints, tinder boxes or candles so that they had some form of light to cheer them along. We can find our little lights too; the comfort of friends, the sympathy of others who have experienced our problems, our faith in God's protection and guidance even though we may feel that we are separated from Him, our hope that joy and happiness will return, as indeed it will if we are determined to find it again.

It is a wonderful experience when the end of the tunnel is reached. At first, we see only a tiny light ahead, as small as a pin point. We recover from depression slowly, but we begin to recognise that life is gradually becoming easier. Perhaps we find that we have laughed, or noticed the beauty of a flower, or felt the stirring of some emotion in a mind that had felt dead for so long. Then the light grows brighter until, at last, we have emerged into full sunshine, the horses are waiting to take over, and the tunnel is behind us. I imagine those old leggers would have celebrated with a draught of ale or whatever they drank in those days. We too will feel great joy when the weary days of depression are over, and we will undoubtedly appreciate life and happiness so much more. Having experienced the dark canal tunnel with its enclosing walls and realised that it was simply part of the journey, I think that we should regard depression in this way. It may be, for us, a necessary part of our journey through life.

The story is told of a conjuror who held up a large white handkerchief. Near the middle of it was a small black spot. 'What can you see?' he asked his audience. 'A black spot,' called out several. 'How strange', said the conjuror, 'didn't anyone notice the large white handkerchief?' Too often, we see the bad things in life far more clearly than the good. If we have learned how to cope with depression, if we believe that it will eventually pass and that light will be there at the end of the tunnel, we too will see the small black spot as only an insignificant part of our lives, not an overwhelming disaster. By believing in hope we will be able to escape from the darkness into the beauty and joy of the sunlight that awaits us.

12. People don't Understand Me

It is very hurtful to feel that we are being unappreciated, rejected or that our good intentions are completely misinterpreted. It is natural enough to resent this, but if we react by withdrawing into ourselves or by adopting a hostile and unfriendly attitude to others in return, we can only worsen the situation. Other people will judge us by our actions which, it is said, speak louder than words; they cannot really understand fully our entire character. After all, there are times when we scarcely understand ourselves. So long as we are honest with ourselves and act in the way that we believe to be right, the opinions of others matter very little and we must not allow ourselves to be unduly influenced by them.

When I was at school I remember learning about detached coefficients during an algebra lesson. It struck me as an amusing expression. I imagined the numbers asserting their independence by casting off their too-clinging associates. Detachment, however, is sometimes a serviceable quality. It will help us to disregard adverse criticism if we can separate ourselves from it, stop brooding about it and put it out of our minds.

Let us imagine a group of knights attacking a hostile city. Arrows and stones rain down on them, but they are unharmed because of their protective armour. Then picture a man riding with them in his ordinary clothes. How much more likely he is to be a victim, and how, without doubt, the enemy will select him as their target.

This is exactly how we feel if we are too sensitive to the criticisms of others.

What can we do about this vulnerability? If we look at the world of nature we see that the soft-bodied animals very often have a protective shell which shields them from harm. This is true of many sea creatures, as well as such animals as snails and tortoises. Others, if they are weak and non-aggressive, find their refuge in strong and secure hiding places. We too must try to form some sort of protective layer to prevent our being too sensitive.

Even more harmful, though, than being too thin skinned, is when we build up resentment because of the way in which others have treated us. At the beginning of the last war, when I was in my late teens, I had just started work and our office was moved out of London into the north of England, where I found accommodation with several other girls in a boarding house close to the sea. While we were there we had quite a frightening experience.

The house was a large, old one and our bedrooms on the upper storeys, the better lower rooms being reserved for holiday guests. In the cold winter evenings we used to gather round a big fire in the lounge, which the kindly landlady would pile high with coal. It was quite by chance one morning, when cleaning the hearth, that she noticed to her surprise how warm it was, though the fire had long since gone out. She called her husband to investigate, he brought in workmen to prise up the floorboards, and at once the room filled with smoke. The hearth had been cracked for some time, sparks must have found their way through, and for weeks the thick wooden beams below the floor had been slowly smouldering away, growing hotter all the time, and were on the point of bursting into flames. There was no fire escape. Had this actually happened at night, no doubt many of us would have been trapped in our rooms.

I have often thought that the most dangerous fires are like this. They smoulder quietly inside, but on the surface they appear to be out until the flames suddenly burst through with tremendous impetus.

Resentment can be very like this, especially if we have not given vent to our feelings, but have pushed them down below the surface of our minds. It can happen so easily. We may have to care for an elderly or sick relative. Because we are fond of them we do not want to hurt them by complaining about the extra burden of work, or their irritating habits or constant demands on our time. Or we may have been treated unjustly at work, or by a friend, and we have been unable to forget the hurtful incident. Perhaps we have had to cope with a bereavement and to avoid upsetting others have refused to give way to grief, throwing ourselves into new activities and trying to blot out past memories. We cannot succeed in this. All we do is to shut our emotions into ourselves and cover them up in the same way that a fire can be dampened down on the surface. The result of this is not only to prevent the fire from going out, but to increase the heat at its centre. And just as fire will suddenly erupt, fiercer than ever, so those emotions will gather strength until they cannot be held down any longer and we break down completely, or plunge into depression, or lose control of ourselves in some other way.

A volcano acts in a similar fashion, suddenly and forcefully throwing out its fire. This, I suppose, is why, when our control snaps and we fly into a rage, we say that we 'blew our top'. The best way of controlling our emotions then is not by suppressing them, but by trying to release them and cool them down. We may find ourselves in intolerable situations which cannot be changed. Naturally we feel resentment, frustration, anger or grief. We have to let these emotions come to the surface, but at the same time use and channel them in such a way that they do not cause harm to ourselves or others.

Anger and frustration can often be worked out by indulging in something as energetic as possible. There are plenty of ways to do this. Taking part in some sport means that we can vent our fury on a cricket or tennis ball and derive a lot of satisfaction from hitting it as hard and often as we can. Tearing up newspapers, digging vigorously in the garden, thumping out loud music on the piano, chopping firewood, smashing old crockery, even punching a cushion or kicking a pillow are all harmless ways of relieving pent-up feelings. If we feel like screaming, we should find an isolated spot and do just that. Some of the most popular stalls at fairs and fêtes are those where we can smash up pots, hit an Aunt Sally, hammer nails into wood or knock down coconuts. This legitimate violence does answer a need for many of us, for it provides an excellent release for accumulated rage or discontent.

If we are very angry with someone and write a letter telling them just what we think of them, it is better not to post it straight away. The act of writing it may well relieve our feelings, but if we re-read it the next day we may then also be able to see the other person's point of view and, having got the resentment out of our system, may even see the funny side of it. Quite likely we will then tear the letter up and forget the whole matter.

The very worst thing to do is to nurse feelings of resentment or frustration. These feelings, if pushed down inside us will not go away. They will grow and fester and can bring us nothing but harm. Emotions, like fire, can be very destructive. We must be able to control them and not allow them to take charge of us.

However, although we should try to forget our resentments and not dwell on other people's opinions of us, we cannot live fulfilled lives if we detach ourselves completely and remain isolated and aloof from our fellows. It is a question of getting our priorities right. First we need to be certain of own integrity, then we must reach out to cooperate with others. A Jewish proverb expresses this:

If I am not for myself, who will be?
But if I am only for myself, what good am I?

We should, I think, accept ourselves and then forget

ourselves. Whether people really understand us or not is unimportant. To find happiness we have to be able to relate to others and be more concerned with their needs and feelings than our own. A modern hymn, based on a prayer of St Francis of Assisi, asks:

> Lord, grant that I may never seek to be
> So much to be consoled as to console,
> To be understood as to understand,
> To be loved as to love with all my soul.

If we can base our lives on these words, we will cease to be troubled by hurt feelings and resentments and will find, as a result, that our lives will be far more contented and satisfying.

13. There is so much Evil in the World

On my way home from shopping one day I went through a quiet park and sat down on a bench to rest for a while. A number of small children were playing on the grassy bank just below me, some rolling down the slope with much gleeful shouting and laughter, while a smaller group at one side were busily engaged in picking daisies and threading them into a chain. Life for them was uncomplicated and carefree; as yet they knew nothing of the troubles, anxieties, threats and traumas of adulthood.

We cannot escape from or shut our eyes to the presence of evil in the world. Newspaper headlines proclaim fresh horrors each day, we bar our houses against burglary, shun dark alleys for fear of muggers; yet, despite all our precautions, cannot tell what ills may befall us or protect ourselves from the sudden onslaught of disease or from a tragic breakdown in family life. At times we find it hard to understand why there should be so much evil, cruelty, pain and suffering.

We inhabit a world which is unutterably beautiful, but that same nature which has created the delicate harebell and the soaring mountain peak allows parasites to burrow into the living flesh of animals, drought, flood and fire to bring painful or lingering death to countless creatures, and excessive cold or heat to maim and destroy the very life which she has brought into being. Can there, after all, be any purpose in this? Is it true, as we have been told, that man has been evolving through the ages, becoming slowly more civilised, understanding more of God and of his own

destiny? We know only too well, when we look at the state
of the world today, at the horrifying forces of destruction
built up by man himself, at the oppression and hatred,
distrust and enmity among the nations, how far we are
from a perfect world.

Some indeed have said, 'How can there be a God, when
so much is wrong with the earth? If He existed He would
not have allowed these things to happen.' And many reject
Him angrily when tragedy and sorrow come into their own
lives.

If seems to me that this sort of criticism completely
misunderstands the nature of God. How thankful we
should be that He is not a sort of puppet manipulator,
moving us across the stage of life regardless of our wishes
or feelings. It is an indication of the extent of His love and
care for us that He limits Himself to working through us,
and then only insofar as we will allow Him, permitting us
to be co-workers with Him, and not mindless slaves. That
we often choose to work against Him and thwart His will
is the price He has been willing to pay for giving us this
precious freedom. We have learnt to prize freedom and to
pity those who live in countries where all activity is con-
trolled by the State, and where it is necessary to suppress
individual thoughts and opinions if they conflict with
those of the authorities. Men have imposed these restrictions on themselves. God allows us freedom to live as we
choose. It is 'man's inhumanity to man' that lies at the bottom of much of the world's suffering.

Whether or not we believe in God, we cannot deny the
existence of evil. Cruelty, greed, envy, lust, pride and
selfishness bring pain and sorrow in their train, and
mankind must bear the responsibility for this. We
sometimes say that nature is cruel, but this is not so.
Cruelty enjoys inflicting pain: nature only destroys in
order that one organism may survive, even if it has to be
at the expense of another. Earthquakes, floods, and
droughts are natural events caused by chemical reactions;
they are very different from the destruction which men

deliberately set out to achieve by war, enslavement, torture, exploitation and domination to gratify their own desires. We can, therefore, say that man has brought much of the suffering in the world upon himself.

But not all of it. So often it is the innocent who suffer, and we complain to God about the injustice of this. Children and babies have done no wrong. Why do they suffer and die? What of the problems of disease which causes world-wide distress? Man has not, in most cases, been responsible for this, and, indeed, is labouring ceaselessly to eradicate it and to heal the sick.

For many centuries, and certainly in Biblical times, men saw suffering of all kind as a punishment meted out by God, a just retribution for the evil-doing of men. God was regarded as being vindictive, jealous and cruel. Men obeyed Him out of fear, and sought to appease His anger by sacrifices and by gifts of the produce of their labours. An even more repugnant belief was that children would suffer for the wrong-doing of their parents, 'unto the third and fourth generation', said the Old Testament. Jesus denied this doctrine. When friends of a blind man asked Him whether it was his own or his parents' sin which had caused his loss of sight, Jesus replied, "His blindness has nothing to do with his sins or his parents' sins. He is blind so that God's power might be seen at work in him." (*Good News Bible*)

Of course, there are some illnesses which we do bring upon ourselves, but it is abundantly clear from the New Testament that illness is never the will of God for us, nor is it inflicted on us by Him. On the other hand, although faith will sometimes cure sickness, we may have to accept it as a necessary experience of life, and we cannot expect God to exempt us from every unpleasant occurrence.

Pain and suffering must be a part of life. As Job said, "Man is born unto trouble as the sparks fly upward". Why must this be? We rebel against it violently when we are young. We look for pleasure and happiness and we try to shut our eyes to death, destruction and disease. We find ourselves embarrassed if we are confronted by people with crippled bodies or minds. As we grow older we find that, try as we may, we cannot escape the burdens of pain and sorrow. Some become embittered by them, some try to get others to carry the load, but sooner or later we have to face our problems alone. We do not keep the robust energy and arrogant confidence of youth. We learn the limitations of our bodies, the frailties of those in whom we had trusted, the pains of failed ambition, disillusionment, lost opportunity, bereavement, and others' ingratitude, deceit and indifference. It is then that, like Job, we cry out, 'Why? Why were we born?'

When I was young so much in life seemed incomprehensible. I would pray for understanding and would listen eagerly to sermons, hoping to be told the secret that would unravel the mystery of life. It was many years before I realised that understanding others can only come when we have been alongside them in their suffering and have experienced it for ourselves. We may read countless books on sociology, psychology and theology and be no nearer a solution. Parents try in vain to protect their children from making the same mistakes as themselves. We learn only by experience, and this I believe is the purpose of life. And God, in the person of His Son, has experienced every kind of sorrow and pain that we may be exposed to. Because of this we can be certain that He understands and suffers with us and is able to bring us comfort and healing.

Very often we find we can endure suffering ourselves with stoicism and be determined to rise above bodily weakness and disability. Everyone has heard of those who have learned to paint or write using their feet or mouths and whose work surpasses that of many of their able-bodied colleagues. Blind people and those confined to wheelchairs sometimes amaze us by their cheerfulness, resourcefulness and courage. Human nature can be ennobled by adversity. But by far the worst pain we have to endure is to see the suffering and distress of those we love. It is at these times that we rebel at the injustice of it and question God's goodness and love.

A friend of mine, whose young baby had suddenly and inexplicably died, told me how difficult she was finding it to believe that God could not in some way have prevented this seemingly meaningless tragedy. Why had the baby been born at all? It is almost impossible for us, with our limited understanding of life's purposes, to find a satisfactory answer. I do not believe that the baby was lost. I think that he had needed to be given life, and that his life would be continued in some way that is outside our human experience. We cannot expect, I think, to comprehend God's whole plan, for our life here must be only a tiny part of it.

I once read of an incident in the life of the artist Michelangelo which helped me to see this more clearly. He had been working, perched on a high scaffolding, on his masterpiece the wonderful ceiling of the Sistine Chapel in Rome, and the huge undertaking was almost completed. A young apprentice, who had been helping him to mix his colours, was on the platform with him. Michelangelo decided to stand back a little from his work in order to obtain a clearer view. He began to move backwards, not realising how close he was to the edge of the scaffolding. The apprentice saw with horror that if his master took one more step he would crash to his death below. A shout would only startle him and precipitate the fall. The young man, with great presence of mind, flung his dripping brush at the painting and a daub of colour streaked across the wonderful ceiling. With a cry of dismay and fury Michelangelo leaped forward and out of danger to protect his precious work. It was only then that he appreciated that by an apparent act of mindless destruction the apprentice had saved his master's life. The painting was easily restored. Perhaps in our lives what sometimes seems to be a disaster is, in fact, necessary for our ultimate well being. We cannot see into the future, just as Michelangelo was completely unaware of the danger he was in.

However much we try, we cannot understand fully why these things should be. We see only events which belong to our earth and our limited existence here. All we can do is to try to endure such pain and suffering as is our lot, and endeavour to lessen the burdens of our fellows.

Because we have free will, we can use the experience of suffering as we choose. We can rage against God and deny His existence; we can react with bitterness and resentment, shutting ourselves away from others and nursing our grievances; or we can make ourselves a burden to our families and friends by magnifying our disabilities and constantly complaining. These are negative reactions. But I believe that everything in life has a positive side and that we can find purpose and meaning even in life's sorrows. Only those who have suffered are able to truly understand and help others in the same situation. Suffering changes us; whether for the better or the worse is for us to decide. It can make life's meaning clearer and bring us closer to God.

Robert Browning wrote:

> Then welcome each rebuff
> That turns earth's smoothness rough...

He was able to see that it is possible to transform evil into good and to find virtue and purpose even in suffering. The supreme example of this was, of course, in the crucifixion of Jesus. If life was effortless and completely carefree, we should become indolent and selfish; courage only develops in the face of pain and danger, gentleness when there is the need to protect, patience when we have learned to endure, and sympathy when we have experienced the depths of the sorrows of others. It must be that our lives are part pleasure and part pain, for both are needed for full growth into maturity. Plants flourishing in lush and fertile soil usually produce more leaves than flowers; the loveliest blooms are often found growing in the most adverse conditions.

The Nazi concentration camps of the last world war were places where evil abounded. Ravensbruck, where

92,000 women and children died, was the most infamous of all. Yet it was here that a prayer was found written on a scrap of wrapping paper near the body of a dead child:

> O Lord, remember not only the men and women of goodwill, but also those of illwill. But do not only remember all the suffering they have inflicted on us. Remember the fruits we bought, thanks to this suffering; our comradeship, our loyalty, our humility, the courage, the genorosity, the greatness of heart which has grown out of all this; and when they come to judgement, let all the fruits that we have borne be their forgiveness.

We tend to picture evil as darkness and goodness as light. Yet sometimes darkness has its rightful place. There is a saying, 'There are dark shadows on earth, but its lights are stronger in contrast.' Night is necessary to give us better rest after the labour of the day; bulbs stored in the dark will grow stronger roots; photographs can be developed and the beauty and wonder of the stars observed. Darkness can be friendly after all if we can overcome our fear of it. It is the dark sweet pea which enhances the more delicately tinted flowers, the black background which brings out bright colours in a picture. When I am on holiday in the Lake District I have noticed that it is the shadows from clouds which make the beautiful effects of light and shade on the fells and lakes. 'All sun makes a desert', and it may be that we need to have some darkness in our lives. The important thing is how we react to it.

Because most evil is of human origin it is surely our responsibility to try to counteract it by putting back into life all we can that is good, constructive and worthwhile. We must concentrate on the positive rather than the negative and seek to cheer and encourage others. I saw a carsticker recently which read: 'Happiness is contagious: be a carrier.'

For if there is evil in the world there is also far much

more that is good and beautiful. We have only to look around us and we can glimpse beauty everywhere. The countryside reveals a constantly changing panorama as the seasons pass; the delicate tracery of twigs and tree branches in winter, a drift of bluebells in spring, the sudden revelation of a bright patch of poppies in a summer cornfield, and the rich russet and gold of woods in autumn. The smallest garden or window box can overflow with wonder, and nature will mercifully cover many of the worst horrors brought about by man. After the last war, jagged, gaping bomb craters in many a city were quickly covered over by the rosebay willow herb, whose bright, prolific flowers hid from sight the ugliness below them.

It is sad, though, that many seem to have no appreciation of the beauty that surrounds them. A glorious sunset will leave them unmoved; they will drive through a breathtaking landscape and be unaware of it, intent only on reaching their journey's end. It is said of Dr Samuel Johnson that once, while he was touring Scotland, he was asked if he did not think the views magnificent. "What views?" he queried. "I can scarcely see a thing: the hills completely shut out the scenery."

So, if we become discouraged at the thought of so much evil, let us not forget that goodness far outweighs it and that light must always overcome darkness. It is a comforting thought that 'there is not enough darkness in the whole world to extinguish the light of one small candle'.

14.   Life's not worth Living: I'd like to End it all

The thought of suicide is the ultimate negation of hope; the rejection of life itself. It is the stage reached when love, joy, pleasure, beauty, friendship, contentment, peace of mind and achievement have all faded, leaving nothing but a blank expanse, a weary and purposeless continuing of existence. Many are driven to this point by extreme sorrow, prolonged ill-health, deepening depression, or burdens and problems which seem to have no solution. It is then that it can seem quite logical to terminate a life which can offer only unending pain and misery. Despite this, I do not believe that suicide can ever be the right answer. Whatever the circumstances, however great the distress, hope is never completely extinguished.

When we reach the point of longing to die we are in a state of depression. Our thoughts have concentrated on the negative and evil aspects of life. It is said that those who take their own lives do so when the balance of their minds is disturbed, and this is nearly always true. Depression pushes us onto a downward slope; the very word describes this lowering of spirits. Although we feel that we are thinking rationally, this is far from the case. Indeed, it is unreasonable to suppose that by terminating our lives we shall also bring to an end the fears and worries that beset us. We need to consider this carefully. I do not believe that suicide is wicked or even cowardly; on the contrary, it takes considerable courage. Neither would I condemn anyone for taking such an action, for how can I know the burden they have to bear?; but I am quite certain that it is the wrong course to take.

When we are depressed, weary and over-burdened we should never trust our feelings. An exhausted brain gives us false messages of guilt, unhappiness and self-loathing. These are symptoms of a troubled mind and in time they will pass.

Suicide tempts us because it offers oblivion; no more need to go on struggling. It is as if we were saying, 'Stop the world. I want to get off'. We suppose that death will be endless sleep; a dissolving into nothingness. But can we be sure of this? It is certainly open to question. To my mind, it is far more reasonable to suppose that our personalities will continue beyond death, and, if this is the case, we would carry those unsolved problems with us.

When I was teaching and the children were preparing for their Sports Day the first thing I taught them was that they must always finish the race, come what may. "Never mind if you can't skip", I told them. "Just go on as best you can until you reach the finishing line. Someone must be last. If it is you it doesn't matter, but it does matter if you give up half way." Life is like a race, and for some it is easier than others. We cannot all be good runners. We may trip and stumble, we may lag far behind, but it is expected of us that we should go on until we reach the finishing line. Suicide is opting out halfway along the course. It is always admitting failure, and as it will spoil a child's race, so it will be cutting short the purpose of our life in this world. It may even be that, if we give up, we must return and live out another human existence in order to fulfil that purpose.

Even if death does bring oblivion, suicide will cause far greater pain and distress than a natural bereavement to those who are close to us. Most suicidal people feel unwanted, unloved and utterly alone; yet this is scarcely ever true. When we are depressed we cannot feel or respond to the love of others. A few years ago I attended the funeral service of a girl who had felt desperately lonely and had finally taken her life. The little church was so packed with mourners that extra chairs had to be brought in, and many there felt deep sorrow at her tragically early death. Her family, friends and neighbours had been far more concerned for her than she had ever realised in her lifetime.

Of course, there can be times in life when our sorrows do seem to be unbearable and it is almost impossible to carry on. In my own time of deep despair I seemed to lose the normal instinct of self-preservation which we all possess. I forgot to look before crossing roads, and once nearly stepped off a fast-moving bus. I heard someone shout, "Look out!", but merely thought that it didn't really matter in the least. I was not deliberately trying to end my life, but I suppose that my subconscious thought was that there was no point in its continuance.

If thoughts of suicide come, if we feel desperate and despairing, we need to seek help and take some positive action. The Samaritans are always available at any hour of the day or night, and it really does help to talk about our troubles to someone else. Sympathetic friends will listen, even if they cannot solve our troubles.

It is often a good idea to write down worries and problems, for this will enable us to get them more into proportion. To engage in something active, such as taking a long walk, is far better than sitting indoors and brooding over our sorrows and cares. If burdens feel beyond our strength to bear we must certainly seek relief, but suicide is not a solution; it is an opting out. We have to look for help, delegate tasks which we are unable to continue with, be content to plod on for a while taking life at a slower pace, and try to set aside unnecessary fears and anxieties.

It may well seem that life is not worth living. We must accept this, for we cannot expect happiness as being ours by right. But if we struggle on as best we may, living just one day at a time, we will find that we are, after all, managing to cope with those tasks which were looming ahead of us as frighteningly as did the labours of Hercules.

In that ancient legend Hercules was set tasks so formidable that they appeared to be utterly impossible. But he succeeded in completing them by refusing to admit that they WERE impossible. He tackled them steadily and patiently, one by one, until he had worked his way through them all to victory.

This is how we must grapple with those feelings of weakness and impotence when we are tempted to give up altogether. We should bear in mind that we are far stronger than we think. It is only our depressed and fearful thoughts which make us feel so helpless and disorientated. A delicate and fragile snowdrop can withstand fierce winter gales, bitter cold and thick snow. The life force in each of us can overcome tremendous odds.

When we feel that we cannot cope with life, it will become less formidable if we can take it in only small portions. Time, after all, is already conveniently divided up for us into years, months, weeks and days. Let us, therefore, limit our thoughts and our efforts to one day only, and resolutely determine to think no further ahead. When we wake in the morning we must not allow our thoughts to dwell on what may happen next week or even tomorrow. We should concentrate on today only, refusing even to consider anything more than twelve hours ahead.

I discovered some words recently which enlarge on this concept:

JUST FOR TODAY

Just for today I will try to live for this day only, and not tackle my whole life problem at once. I can do something for twelve hours that would appal me if I felt I had to keep it up for a lifetime.

Just for today I will be happy. After all, most people are about as happy as they make their minds to be.

Just for today I will try to strengthen my mind. I will learn something useful. I will read something that requires effort, thought and concentration.

Just for today I will adjust myself to what is, and I will not keep trying to adjust everything else to my own desires.

Just for today I will exercise my soul three ways: I will do somebody a good turn, and not get found out. I will do at least two things I don't want to do – just for exercise. And today, if my feelings are hurt, I will not show it to anyone.

Just for today I will look as agreeable as I can, dress becomingly, speak low, act courteously, criticise not one bit, and try not to improve anybody except myself.

Just for today I will have a programme. I may not follow it exactly, but I will have it. I will save myself from two pests; hurry and indecision.

Just for today I will be unafraid. Especially I will not be afraid to enjoy what it beautiful, and to believe that, as I give to the world, so the world will give to me.

The words of a familiar hymn also echo these thoughts:

> Lord, for tomorrow and its need I do not pray,
> So keep me, guide me, guard me, Lord
> Just for today.

But sometimes to keep going on, even for one day, can seem beyond our power. When troubles overwhelm us we are like children lost in the dark, alone and afraid, not knowing which way to turn. During the war, I was working in a government department and our office was in a large hotel in Southport, near to the main road. We worked until late every night and always carried torches on our way home, because of the blackout. One night I came out of the hotel alone and my torch battery failed halfway through the shrubbery which I had to cross before reaching the road. It was like being in a maze. There seemed to be paths in all directions, but I could not discover the right one. I could faintly hear the traffic on the road, but, of course, because of the war regulations there were no headlamps or street lights. I knew that somewhere a path led out of the bushes, but it seemed that I would never find it. When I returned to work the next morning and saw the shrubbery in daylight, I was astonished to realise how small it really was, and how simple a matter it should have been to reach the road from the hotel. Years later, when I was deeply depressed, I remembered that lost feeling. Problems can appear to have no solution. We feel that life has become an impossible muddle and that there is no way out of it. The sense of being lost is very real and very frightening.

But we need to realise that just as there must be a path out of a maze, so there is a way out of our troubles. The feeling that we can never escape from them in all illusion caused by our depression itself.

I have sometimes seen a very small baby being carried on a bus or train. It looks about it, and its eyes are round with wonder. I have often thought how bewildering it must find its surroundings; most of the things is sees can have no meaning to it. But human babies and newly born animals are not afraid of the strange world in which they find themselves. They are reassured by the presence of the mother in whose body they have been carried and whose arms now enfold and protect them. So they wonder, but do not fear. If we have a belief in God's care and protection of us we are similarly comforted. We do not always understand the things that happen to us in life, but we need not fear them.

The important thing is to keep plodding on, even when life seems intolerable. You probably know the story of the two frogs that strayed into a dairy and fell into a large bowl of cream. They swam round and round in it but were unable to climb out because the sides of the bowl were too slippery. Time passed and they grew more and more exhausted. One felt that his efforts were useless and gave up the struggle. He sank to the bottom and was drowned. The other, though he could see no point in continuing to swim, refused to give up hope. He continued to churn up the cream with his strong back legs as he circled the bowl. A mound of butter gradually formed as a result of his exertions, and presently, to his astonishment, he found that his feel were able to gain a hold and he managed to escape. If we keep in mind that it is the very fact of keeping on, even when no result can be seen, which in the end brings about a cure, we will find that life eventually becomes easier.

Let us realise that if thoughts of suicide come into our minds, seeming to promise an easy means of escape, they are misleading and spurious. In Spencer's 'Faerie Queene' it was the false and treacherous Archimago who lured the Red Cross Knight into his cave and, in the guise of a friend, offered him a rope, poison, a dagger and other means of self-destruction as the most sensible way out of his troubles.

We so easily lose sight of the fact that our lives are not our own, but are given to us on trust. We cannot live them in complete isolation; so many of our words and actions have far-reaching consequences that we may never be aware of, and we cannot die without the repercussions of our death affecting the lives of a great many others.

While we have life, let us concentrate on living. Countless potential suicides have in later years been profoundly grateful that they did not, in fact, take that step, but were able to go on and find renewed happiness. Life always is worth living, however overshadowed out path may be at times. In George Borrow's book *Lavengro* a gypsy, speaking to a young man who professed to being weary of living, reminded him of the joy and wonder of life:

> There's night and day, brother, both sweet thing; sun, moon and stars, brother, all sweet things; there's likewise a wind on the heath. Life is very sweet, brother; who would wish to die?

15.   I'm Afraid of Death

There is no shame in fearing death; it is a natural reaction. Yet I think for the most part it is a groundless fear. We tend to feel apprehensive when we approach any new experience; when we start school, begin work, enter hospital for an operation, or take our first flight: all these hold possible hazards and dangers; we are leaving familiar routines and entering into unknown territory. Yet, when we look back on these events, we realise that much of that foreboding was misplaced. Far from bringing about dire misfortune, our going forward was of benefit to us. All life is progression from one experience to another; a growth into maturity. Just as children cannot remain in infancy, pleasant though they may find it, so, when our life cycle is completed we cannot cling to an earthly existence, but must go on to the stage that is beyond it.

Can we believe, though, that there is anything beyond death? There would surely be no point to life at all if, when we die, that was the end of it, that so much pain, effort, the struggle to understand and the learning gained by experience were snuffed out, like a candle, in death. To me, it can only make any sort of sense if our life spent on earth is just a small fraction of our existence, a preparatory school, perhaps, which equips us for the university of the wider realities ahead. It seems inconceivable that a lifetime of accumulated knowledge should be thrown onto the rubbish heap when we die.

The eager, thrusting, all-pervading energy of life would be futile were it to end in annihilation. The earth, indeed, may return to that state of barren lifelessness which was found on the moon and which almost certainly characterises our nearest planets; but earth is only the dwelling place of life. It shelters, but has not created it, just as our bodies are the vehicles which contain our living selves, but are discarded on death.

Human life is a mystery. We know so much and yet, when we look up into the night sky and see the countless stars above us, we realise that our sum of knowledge is miniscule. We notice a stream flowing quietly by. It has washed over those stones for centuries. Roman soldiers may have crossed the very boulders we gaze at now. The same stones were there, the same sun shone down on them, the same hills rose behind them. But where were we then? In another hundred years time the stream will be lapping over those identical rocks. Will we be able to see it then? We read of people in history. They felt as we do now, had similar worries and fears, loved, wept, laughed and gossipped. They have gone. We too will have our brief span of life and then our bodies will grow old and die. We are conscious, as we grow older, that our real self does not age; the body becomes less agile, it no longer serves us so well, but our thoughts and feelings are as they were in our youth. We can leap in spirit; love with as great an intensity. We realise with a greater clarity that out bodies are but an outer clothing, and so we wonder, 'From whence did I come? To what do I go?'

I have sometimes heard people say, 'I'm not afraid of dying, but I fear the pain'. This is nearly always an unnecessary fear. We all experience some pain in life. Most illnesses involve suffering, but when they have run their course the pain disappears. Death is often completely painless and, when it comes naturally, is usually preceded by unconsciousness, during which the organs of the body gradually slow down as their work is done. Even those who remain conscious until death almost always experience a quiet, pain-free period at the end when life slips gently away. Dante wrote:

> So just as a good mariner when he draws near to the harbour lets down his sails, and enters it gently with slight headway on; so we ought to let down the sails of our worldly pursuits, and turn to God with all our understanding and heart, so that we may come to that haven with all composure and with all peace. And our own nature gives us a good lesson in gentleness, in so far as there is in such a death no pain, nor any bitterness; but as a ripe apple lightly and without violence detaches itself from its bough, so our soul severs itself without suffering from the body where it has dwelt.

Death is an intrinsic part of life: we cannot have life without death. As trees shed their leaves at the approach of winter, so we, in due course, reach the end of our life cycle. Death is as natural as birth or as sleep for, as the Bible tells us, "To everything there is a season and a time to every purpose under the heaven; a time to be born, and a time to die."

Because medical science has eradicated so much disease, people today have a longer expectancy of life than in the past. However, to aim towards progressively lengthening man's life span, as if we should desperately seek to ward off death as the ultimate enemy for as long as possible, is, I feel, misguided. Death comes frequently as a friend, for as our bodies age our hold on life loosens and the duties, pressures and strains of living weigh upon us ever more heavily until death is seen as a release. I once read a story by Edgar Allen Poe of a man who so feared dying that he sought out an acquaintance possessed of supernatural powers who was able to take from him the ability to die. He grew old and ill. Time passed and his bodily state continued to deteriorate until he found himself yearning for that very death which he had so much dreaded.

We cannot remain indefinitely on earth. Our time here

is only a brief interlude, or as Wordsworth said ". . . . . .a sleep and a forgetting. The soul that rises with us, our life's star, hath elsewhere its setting, and cometh from afar." To stay for ever on earth would be to seek to retain the adolescent in the kindergarten. The destiny of man is not within the confines of the earth, but extends far beyond it.

We cannot know when we will die: this we must leave in God's hands. It has been said, 'I am immortal till my work is done'. But we do not need to worry about how to die, and more that we need to be concerned with how to sleep. We lie down at night and sleep comes naturally, as does our awakening to the new day. If life is seen as a journey, then death is only a change of train and the journey goes on. Dying must surely be very like birth. In death, as in birth, we will be protected, guided and received with love and care into the new life which awaits us.

When a rocket is launched into space it is accompanied of the first stage of its flight by a small booster rocket, the function of which is to thrust it away from the earth's atmosphere. When this is accomplished the booster rocket is discarded. It falls away; its purpose achieved. When the time comes for us to die we are able to discard our bodies in a similar way. Their part has been to enable us to live in the atmosphere of the earth, breathing its air, absorbing its food, moving from place to place, seeing, hearing, understanding and touching the things which belong to the earth. We inhabit our bodies, we need them while we remain on earth, but they are disposable and unnecessary when we travel further on our journey.

As we grow older we often find that the ties which hold us to the earth seem to be loosening. Perhaps many of our friends and our family have already died, we do not enjoy earth's pleasures as much as in former years, and we feel ourselves out of tune with the changing world of the young. Even so, it is natural enough to be reluctant to leave all the familiar sights, the beauty and the happiness that we have known on earth. When we draw near to death we may well, as Gray said, "cast a longing, lingering look behind". But we have not reached the end of a blind alley. We are journeying on, not alone, but in the company of all who have lived on earth. J. M. Barrie pictured this when he wrote:

> One who dies is only a little ahead of the procession all moving that way. When we round the corner we will see him again. We have only lost him for a moment because we fell behind stopping to tie a shoelace.

Where then are we going? What is beyond this world of time, and what happens when we die? This, of course, we do not know. Just as we do not remember our birth, so we cannot project our consciousness beyond the moment of death. Many ideas have been put forward, but we have no way of proving them. The notion of an insubstantial shade or ghost drifting aimlessly around its old familiar haunts is a primitive one. The Ancient Greeks thought of the Underworld, the place of departed spirits, as a dark and gloomy realm peopled by wistful shadows. Spiritual life is on a higher plane than ours and we must surely expect it to bring new experiences; not a pale imitation of earthly existence.

We speak of heaven and eternity, but these are such abstract ideas that we can scarcely give them any substance. We are in a similar position to an ant asked by its fellows to describe the human way of life. Were it to enter a house it would be totally incapable of understanding the purpose of anything it saw; a floor would be an arid desert, a rug an impenetrable jungle, and kitchen equipment wholly meaningless fabrications. So it is with us. We can only assess and make judgements with our human brains and they know only the things which appertain to our own world.

But, because we believe that God's dwelling is in heaven and that, after death, we shall enter it ourselves, we cannot help but conjecture what life in heaven might involve. We are often baffled by accounts in the Bible of heavenly visions, simply, I suppose, because our language has no words to describe what was seen. Pictures of angels with harps seated on clouds are but childish imaginings, and many of the questions we ask about heaven arise from our utter incomprehension. We say, 'Where is heaven?' because we feel we should be able to place it somewhere within the universe; above the sun, perhaps, or just beyond the planets. People even said, when space travel first became a reality, that they could no longer believe in God because no sign of Him or of heaven was discovered 'out there'. Heaven being 'above the deep blue sky' is an elementary idea which has now been rejected by most thinking people, for why should heaven be 'up' or 'down' or, indeed, in any specific place, as if it were merely an as yet undiscovered continent?

When we read the account of the Ascension we find the expression, "He went UP into heaven." There are two reasons for this. The people who lived when the gospels were written did believe that heaven was situated literally above them, and hell below. Such had been the assumption of mankind since primitive times, probably because men worshipped the sun or the moon and looked up to see them. This is why temples were built as tall as was possible, and may be the reason for the setting up of those huge stone monuments, such as Stonehenge. For hundreds of years churches and cathedrals were given spires or towers soaring upwards and pointing, it was supposed, heavenwards. In the second place, it is natural to think of 'up' as being better: chiefs of old sat on a raised dais, we speak of the Upper House in Parliament, a college of Higher Education or a High School, and of people being at the head of their profession. The very word superior means at a higher level. It is in this sense that we should think of Jesus ascending to heaven, as a child will say that he is going up, when he means into a more senior class at school. Heaven is not so much a place as a state of being.

There are those who find it hard to believe in heaven

because they do not understand how it can contain the countless millions who have lived from the creation of the earth until the present time. But why should we fix limitations? Space and area are, once again, just human conceptions.

Jesus Himself spoke very little about heaven, apart from the parable of Dives and Lazarus, which was set in the pictorial language of those days and was not, I think, intended to be taken literally. He found that even the Pharisees, the religious leaders of His time, failed to understand His teaching, and said to Nicodemus, "If I have told you earthly things, and ye believe not, how shall ye believe if I tell you of heavenly things?" He did, however, say very definitely that life continues after death, though it is a very different life from that which we experience on earth, and He frequently spoke of God as our heavenly Father.

It is natural to wonder what we shall do in heaven. Will we meet friends and relations again? Will there be animals and flowers there? Will there be work to do, things to learn and discover, as on earth? We cannot answer these questions with certainty, though I do believe that we will be reunited with those we have loved on earth. We do know, however, from Jesus' teaching, that life after death will be happy and fulfilled and that it will be "in our Father's house", a lovely description, and another way of saying that we shall be going home to the place where we belong.

To die, we are told, is to enter into eternal life; to exchange mortality for immortality. Eternity and immortality are almost as difficult to comprehend as is the concept of heaven. Our thinking must necessarily be in terms of time, for everything on earth is measured by time; night and day, yesterday, tomorrow, birthdays and festivals, historical events, A.D. or B.C., the seasons which affect the growing of our food, birth, maturity and death; all these are seen in relation to time. In the solar system life is ruled by the sun; once we are outside its influence, time, as we know it, has no meaning, and we can begin to consider its alternative, eternity.

Our bodies have a built-in ageing process with a life expectancy of seventy to eighty years. It is only when we try to imagine existence outside the human body and outside the solar system, or independent of it, that we can begin, albeit dimly, to comprehend eternity. Perhaps the first step towards understanding is to try to enlarge our limited vision. An old story attempts to do this: In the midst of a vast desert stands a block of granite rock. It is one mile high, one mile deep and one mile wide. Once in every hundred years a small bird comes to the rock and sharpens its beak on the granite. When the birds have worn the stone completely away, one day in eternity will have passed.

> Time, like an ever-rolling stream,
> Bears all its sons away.

This gives us a visual impression of the passage of time, which does, indeed, as a moving staircase, carry us inexorably onwards; and we, locked securely to our own step, can neither stand still nor go forwards or backwards at will. Our minds, however, are capable of more than our bodies and may sometimes attempt to overrule time. Memory helps us to bring back and relive the past, selecting those events which we wish to treasure. We prize tape recordings, photographs, or even paintings or souvenirs which preserve pleasurable moments in time. It is possible by concentrating deeply on some beautiful scene or happy experience to impress it so deeply on the memory that it will stay with us. Lines of poetry once learned remain permanently our own.

When we think of God who created time and the universe, we realise that He is outside it and it is only because of our limited understanding that we ask such naive questions as 'Who made God?'. We cannot grasp that there never was a time before God was, because time is only a human conception. God is. It was Plato who first gave us this definition of God by never saying 'God was', or 'God will be'. God is; regardless of passing time. With us there is past and future, but not with God. Moses too gave God the name 'I am', and Jesus outraged the Pharisees and Scribes by telling them, 'Before Abraham was, I am'. I think it is even possible in our prayers to disregard time; to pray, for instance, that someone may be helped through an experience that, for them, is already past.

It is as we grope towards a clearer perception of God that we come closest to finding the meaning of eternity. Hans Andersen, whose children's stories often contained deep truths, made this point in the story of the Snow Queen. The child Kay was only freed from the power of evil when he was able to form, from a confused jumble of ice blocks, the letters of the word 'eternity'.

So when we contemplate death and dying we should view it, not with despair, but with hope. It is but a way leading us from one stage of being to another; like, said Mary Webb, "a gate on the skyline swinging open".

> Life is eternal and love is immortal
> And death is but a horizon and the
> Horizon is but the limit of our sight
> *Abraham Lincoln.*

16. Travelling with Hope

As we travel on our way through life we find that we cannot stand still; we must journey on from day to day. Inevitably the road winds and we cannot see round its twists and turns or over the summits of its hills, but we must trust that good awaits us, and not tread fearfully, anticipating trouble. Cares and sorrows come to all, but when they do we must still go on with a good heart knowing that we will overcome them. For we can do so.

When thoughts of despair come, we need to lift our minds from the worries and anxieties of the moment, and try to absorb ourselves into the beauty of the world about us; to feel the sunshine on our faces, hear the wind in the trees, see the glowing colours of the flowers at our feet. If we envisage our worries in proportion to the great wholeness and perfection of the universe, we realise that, however small and insignificant we may be, we ourselves make up a part of it. For troubles must pass and wounds heal, pain be forgotten and evils eventually overcome, because they will be used for good in the eternal scheme of things. All that has happened to us in our past life will make us stronger and better equipped for the future. Nothing, not even grief, pain or care is meaningless: all, if we will have patience, will yet be well. I came across these words in a little church in Rye, Sussex:

> Upon the wreckage of thy yesterday
>   design the structure of tomorrow.
> Lay strong corner-stones of purpose
>   and prepare

Great blocks of wisdom, cut from past despair.
Shape mighty pillars of resolve, to set
Deep in the tear-wet mortar of regret.
Work on with patience, through thy toil be slow,
Yet day by day thy edifice shall grow.
Believe in God – in thine own self believe –
All thou hast desired thou shalt achieve.

We have to learn to make our thoughts positive, not negative; to look up, not down. When we are depressed and disheartened our heads droop and we drag our feet wearily, but when we travel with hope we stride forward with confidence and our spirits are able to "rise up with wings as eagles".

My mother grew up in a small Cumbrian village among the high fells of the Lake District. As in every village it contained a few eccentric characters, and mother would tell us amusing stories about them when we were children. There was one very rich but elderly and arthritic lady who was confined to a wheelchair. Being of an independent and forceful nature, this by no means restricted her to the house. She would have her chair propelled to the top of a steeply sloping lonnin (the dialect word for a narrow lane). Then she would release the brake and come careering down at breakneck speed, shouting "Look up! Look up!" as she descended, for the benefit of unsuspecting wayfarers who might be making their way up the lonnin. Consequently, this lane became known as 'Look up lonnin'. It conjured up in my mind, every time I heard it mentioned, a delightful picture of this geriatric Jehu in her ricketty Victorian chair enjoying her morning excercise. But this exhortation of hers to look up is worth bearing in mind.

When explorers have to climb a difficult mountain peak or cross a narrow bridge across a deep ravine, the one thing they must never do is to look down. This would reveal to them the dangerous drop below, and they would find themselves thinking of the possibility of falling. The thought would be enough to increase to risk of their doing so. Our minds affect our bodies and can cause them to react in certain ways. So, when we start to lose hope, we are looking down, fearing failure, believing that we cannot go on and that all is lost. It is then that we must try to raise our thoughts and lift them up, telling ourselves over and over again, 'Yes, I can do it. I will not give in.'

We have to search for hope and when we find it, guard and cherish it. For hope is more precious than jewels: if we possess it we need no longer fear any dark places on earth. Recently, a friend sent me a poem which expresses this:

When, long before the dawn
A robin pours his song into the night,
Hope may come sweetly.

When, at approaching spring,
Within the soil life cannot be restrained,
Hope may stir slowly.

And when a sudden shaft of sunlight
Breaks through boughs and strikes a shadowed
     woodland floor,
Hope may come fleetingly.

But when the days are short and winter deep,
It is the season to recall a star that hung above
     a stall
Wherein an infant lay asleep: a newborn baby
     with a wrinkled face,
And then the light of hope into a dark place
Streams eternally.

Doreen Darby.

But perhaps the wisest words on hope are these:

Hope is like the sun
Which, as we travel towards it
Casts our shadow behind us.